Educating Social Entrepreneurs

Educating Social Entrepreneurs

From Idea Generation to Business Plan Formulation

Volume I

Paul Miesing and Maria Aggestam

BEP BUSINESS EXPERT PRESS

Educating Social Entrepreneurs: From Idea Generation to Business Plan Formulation, Volume I

Copyright © Business Expert Press, LLC, 2017.

First published in 2017 by
Business Expert Press, LLC
222 East 46th Street, New York, NY 10017
www.businessexpertpress.com

ISBN-13: 978-1-63157-252-4 (paperback)
ISBN-13: 978-1-63157-253-1 (e-book)

Business Expert Press Principles for Responsible Management Education Collection

Collection ISSN: 2331-0014 (print)
Collection ISSN: 2331-0022 (electronic)

Cover and interior design by Exeter Premedia Services Private Ltd., Chennai, India

First edition: 2017

10 9 8 7 6 5 4 3 2 1

Printed in the United States of America.

Abstract

Educating Social Entrepreneurs: From Idea Generation to Business Plan Formulation appears at the time of unprecedented environmental disasters, natural resources depletion and significant failure of governments and global business to attend social problems occurring around the globe. In the world of downsizing, restructuring and social changes, notions of traditional venture creation and the ways of creating social values have been challenged.

Drawing from contributions by scholars of social entrepreneurship from Europe, North and South America, and Africa, this edited volume reveals interdisciplinarity of entrepreneurship research. To assist the readers, students, and teachers in understanding some dilemmas of our time, the contributors to these collections adopt an array of theoretical frameworks that all examine a multitude of societal and business issues in which the social entrepreneur surfaces.

This Social Entrepreneurship book draws examples from various parts of the global business world and various societies and prepares students, scholars, and entrepreneurial managers to deal with the challenges presented by a new and diverse business environment. It is our belief that these two volumes endorse the importance of social entrepreneurship in the competitive business landscape and prepare students of business and other faculties to create their own business plan for a social venture.

Illuminating troublesome aspects of the global social and business worlds, this Social Entrepreneurship book comprises two volumes and covers key issues such as defining social entrepreneurship; contexts for social entrepreneurship; pitching and communicating social opportunities; and also implementing social opportunities that covers the areas of organizational structures and hybrid organization for social enterprises; mobilizing resources to fund social ventures; scaling the social ventures; and ecopreneuring as social enterprises.

Students, scholars, and entrepreneurs who want to prepare themselves to help the poverty-stricken world and deal with social entrepreneurship will find this to be beneficial reading.

Keywords

case studies, entrepreneurship, social business plan, social entrepreneurship

Contents

Introduction

Paul Miesing

University at Albany, State University of New York

In simple terms, a "social enterprise" is an organization created to have a specific social impact in a financially viable manner by reinvesting its profits in areas that are otherwise outside the conventional economic mainstream. These organizations are becoming increasingly popular and important as disparities increase in wealth, education, employment, clean water and sanitation, health care, technology, affordable and clean energy, and environmental degradation. Moreover, we face one of the greatest challenges the world has ever known: natural resource depletion along with the negative impact of climate change. It is important to note that there has also been significant failure from governments, nongovernment organizations (NGOs), charities, and foundations in meeting these significant societal challenges—so much so that solving them has become a top global priority (United Nations, "Millennium Development Goals," n.d.).

While markets are powerful engines of economic growth, businesses have often been criticized for not doing enough to remedy these problems. For instance, well-established multinational corporations are often unwilling or unable to solve these issues, sometimes on ideological grounds. Even when companies attempted to tackle large societal issues with public services, corporate social responsibility (CSR) programs, or through donations to charities, these efforts were insufficient and even made CSR sound like a cliché. But for social enterprises, value accrues to both society and the economy; hence, they must maximize returns on total social value. Moreover, millennials surveyed said that while they have a positive view of business' role in society, they still want businesses to focus more on people (employees, customers, and society), products, and purpose—and less on profits (Deloitte Millennial Survey 2016).

Many of the markets where social enterprises try to alleviate social problems have constellations of multiple and diverse stakeholders who are willing and able to share in defraying the costs of these transactions. Business strategy guru Michael Porter's description of the principle of shared (not shareholder) value in the *Harvard Business Review* became HBR's "Top Article" of 2011 and one of its 10 "Must Reads": "The opportunity to create economic value through creating societal value will be one of the most powerful forces driving growth in the global economy" (Porter and Kramer 2011). Later that year, Hitt and colleagues similarly wrote about social entrepreneurship (Hitt et al. 2011):

> "… [M]any have argued that entrepreneurial activity is a major contributor to economic development and growth, creating new jobs and enhanced market valuations (Baumol and Strom 2007). Yet entrepreneurial activity can provide other benefits to society as well."

> "A new area of research referred to as social entrepreneurship examines how entrepreneurs develop enterprises with the intent of helping societal members, often those who are underprivileged and have low incomes (Kistruck et al. 2011). This focus has become a significant and growing research area (Short, Moss, and Lumpkin 2009; Zahra et al. 2008). Essentially, social entrepreneurs establish organizations to meet social needs in ways that improve the quality of life and increase human development over time (Zahra et al. 2008) while benefiting owners in ways that continue revenue flow and allow them to earn a return on their investment."

> "… [There are also] attempts to create new companies that enrich the natural environment and/or are designed to overcome or limit others' negative influences on the physical environment. For example, … novel innovations could be used to address a number of environmental problems (Adner and Kapoor 2010). Many firms may take actions to reduce the negative influences their operations typically have on the environment with the hope of creating a positive greening effect (Delmas and Montes-Sancho 2010)."

"Thus, overall entrepreneurial activity can help to build new economic, social, institutional, and cultural environments and thereby provide significant benefits to society (Rindova et al. 2009)."

As a result, social entrepreneurs have emerged by using markets, business techniques, management principles, and private sector practices to solve social/cultural or environmental problems as well as remaining financially viable—the proverbial "triple bottom line" of people, planet, and profits. While noble in purpose, these innovators face inherent disadvantages. Without relying on charities, grants, and donations, these enterprises must develop a sustainable business model that often targets the "bottom of the pyramid" (Prahalad and Hart 2002) requiring innovative solutions and multiple sources of funding (e.g., loans, impact investors, crowdfunding, business plan competitions) and other resources (e.g., time, expertise, networks, volunteers) that are novel yet can be scaled and replicated by others. According to Ashoka, "Social entrepreneurs are individuals with innovative solutions to society's most pressing social problems. They are ambitious and persistent, tackling major social issues and offering new ideas for wide-scale change" ("What is a Social Entrepreneur?" n.d.). Not bound by traditional limits of business ventures, social entrepreneurs succeed by collaborating, being lean ("bricoleur"), managing risks, and creating new ways to measure their impact. Ironically, their approach has migrated to well-established organizations in both the private and public sectors (e.g., such NGOs as BRAC and Oxfam).

This Workbook evolved from a dearth of practical, hands-on, interactive materials for social entrepreneurship—somewhat surprising given the discipline's recent growth in popularity (e.g., Bornstein 2012). For instance, a recent review of social entrepreneurship texts highlights the need for richer pedagogical materials: "instructors and professors are generally left on their own when it comes to activities that emphasize the create level of critical thinking. ... Future editions of these texts could more thoughtfully consider how to include activities that will encourage creating on the part of students" (Moss and Gras 2012). Moreover, there is a tremendous need for cases, examples, and models in the developing world.

This is precisely the purpose of this volume. We organized a workshop in May 2015 *specifically* to develop commentaries that provide background information on a topic, exercises that offer opportunities to experience the topic, and short cases (2 to 5 pages that can be handled within one class hour) that can be used to discuss how to apply the topic. This approach should help aspiring social entrepreneurs create their business plans. We structure this workbook into two volumes based on the topics that emerged from the workshop and resulting submissions: Volume I contains sections on Defining Social Entrepreneurship; Contexts for Social Entrepreneurs; and Recognizing, Pitching, and Communicating Social Opportunities. Volume II is concerned with implementation so covers sections on Organizational Structures and Hybrid Organizations for Social Enterprises; Mobilizing Resources to Fund Social Ventures; Scaling the Social Venture; and Ecopreneuring as Social Enterprises. We also have a variety of resources useful in developing a social business plan, including a worksheet at the end of each section that helps the student reflect on that topic in building their business plan. There is also a template of items to consider in writing that plan as well as a variety of additional resources.

Our hope is that aspiring social entrepreneurs will develop a stronger and more meaningful social enterprise as a result of this volume. We invite readers and users of this Workbook to share their experiences and specially to provide feedback that would be valuable in future revisions and improvements—what works or does not, should items be added or deleted, are there other approaches that should be included?

References

Adner, R., and R. Kapoor. 2010. "Value Creation in Innovation Ecosystems: How the Structure of Technological Interdependence Affects Firm Performance in New Technology Generations." *Strategic Management Journal* 31, no. 3, pp. 306–33.

Baumol, W.J., and R.J. Strom. 2007. "Entrepreneurship and Economic Growth." *Strategic Entrepreneurship Journal* 1, nos. 1–2, pp. 233–37.

Bornstein, D. 2012. "The Rise of the Social Entrepreneur." *New York Times* (November 13) available at http://opinionator.blogs.nytimes.com/2012/11/13/the-rise-of-social-entrepreneur/?_php=true&_type=blogs&_r=0

Delmas, M.A., and M.J. Montes-Sancho. 2010. "Voluntary Agreements to Improve Environmental Quality: Symbolic and Substantive Cooperation." *Strategic Management Journal* 31, no. 6, pp. 575–601.

Deloitte Millennial Survey. 2016. "Millennials Want Business to Shift Its Purpose" available at www2.deloitte.com/global/en/pages/about-deloitte/articles/gx-millennials-shifting-business-purpose.html

Hitt, M.A., R.D. Ireland, D.G. Sirmon, and C.A. Trahms. 2011. "Strategic Entrepreneurship: Creating Value for Individuals, Organizations, and Society." *Academy of Management Perspectives* 25, no. 2, pp. 57–75.

Kistruck, G., J.W. Webb, R.D. Ireland, and C. Sutter. 2011. "Microfranchising in Base-of-the-Pyramid Markets: Institutional Challenges and Adaptations to the Franchise Model." *Entrepreneurship Theory and Practice* 35, no. 3, pp. 503–31.

Moss, T.W., and D. Gras. 2012. "A Review and Assessment of Social Entrepreneurship Textbooks." *Academy of Management Learning & Education* 11, no. 3, pp. 518–27.

Porter, M.E., and M. Kramer. 2011. "Creating Shared Value: How to Fix Capitalism and Unleash a New Wave of Growth." *Harvard Business Review* 89, pp. 62–77.

Prahalad, C.K., and S.L. Hart. 2002. "The Fortune at the Bottom of the Pyramid." strategy+business (January 10) First Quarter/Issue 26 available at www.strategy-business.com/article/11518?gko=9a4ba

Rindova, V., D. Barry, and D.J. Ketchen. 2009. "Entrepreneuring as emancipation." *Academy of Management Review* 34, no. 3, pp. 477–91.

Short, J.C., T.W. Moss, and G.T. Lumpkin. 2009. "Research in Social Entrepreneurship: Past Contributions and Future Opportunities." *Strategic Entrepreneurship Journal* 3, no. 2, pp. 161–94.

United Nations, "Millennium Development Goals" (n.d.) available at www.un.org/millenniumgoals/

"What is a Social Entrepreneur?" available at www.ashoka.org/social_entrepreneur

Zahra, S.A., H.N. Rawhouser, N. Bhawe, D.O. Neubaum, and J.C. Hayton. 2008. "Globalization of Social Entrepreneurship Opportunities." *Strategic Entrepreneurship Journal* 2, no. 1, pp. 117–31.

PART I

Defining Social Entrepreneurship

CHAPTER 1

Social Entrepreneuring: "What's Good for Society Is Also Good for Business"

Maria Aggestam

Sten K. Johnson Centre for Entrepreneurship, Lund University

Introduction

The purpose of this chapter is to address and alert us to the creation of novel entrepreneurial activities, organizations, and companies that stimulate new business development in the poverty-stricken global world and to highlights entrepreneurial practice concerned with contesting climate changes. The Global situation, with its attendant financial crises, significant corporate greed, and ruthless profit-seeking by globalized capitalism with evident environmental disasters, has created a growing concern in various societies. This study explores the potential of social entrepreneurship on two unique and personal platforms. Both platforms illustrate contextually grounded acts which that are also the means by which social entrepreneurship preserves the possibility of change. Both cases give primary emphasis to independent, individual action, and agency that helps us better appreciate the complexity of how entrepreneurial activities are enacted. Consistent with this, each of the cases is located in the wider context of globalized capitalism while focusing on particular issues concerned respectively with wide-reaching conditions of local poverty, contesting climate change and abuse of global natural resource at different levels of society. Emphasis is given to the process of poverty-stricken conditions worldwide and of the fight against the abuse of our shared natural environmental reserves through which social entrepreneurial opportunities are realized.

Is social entrepreneurship critical to addressing the inequalities of the world? Some entrepreneurship researchers have argued that social entrepreneurship is ill-equipped to serve the disadvantaged part of the world population, and also our environment, and therefore cannot change the world for the better. Yet, for some, commercial companies and ruthless profit-seeking by globalized capitalism are close allies. This situation, with its attendant financial crises, significant corporate greed, and growing awareness of environmental disasters, has created a growing market for social entrepreneurship and boosted the attractiveness of social entrepreneurship education. The younger generation has found itself delving deeper into the constituents of global capitalism and is gradually starting to abandon the "dot.com get-rich model" in favor of supporting both social entrepreneurship and socially and environmentally conscious ideals. This study follows in the footsteps of the debate in the academic community and explores the potential of social entrepreneurship on two unique and personal platforms.

Both platforms illustrate contextually grounded acts that are also the means by which social entrepreneurship preserves the possibility of change. Both cases give primary emphasis to independent, individual action and agency that helps us better appreciate the complexity of how entrepreneurial activities are enacted. Consistent with this, each of the cases is located in the wider context of globalized capitalism while focusing on particular issues concerned respectively with wide-reaching conditions of local poverty and contesting climate change and global natural resource abuse at different levels of society. Emphasis is given to the process of poverty-stricken conditions worldwide and of the fight against the abuse of our shared natural environmental reserves through which social entrepreneurial opportunities are realized.

The aim of this study is to address and alert us to the creation of novel entrepreneurial activities, organizations, and companies that stimulate new business development in the poverty-stricken global world and to highlight entrepreneurial practice concerned with contesting climate changes with particular *forward-looking process of imagining* (Ford 2002). Here, social entrepreneurship can be seen in two directions. First, it covers the ways in which extreme poverty in the world can be eliminated by using simple market-based methods and also illustrates the challenges of the self-help model of venture creation for survival. Second, the study identifies and illustrates powerful social entrepreneurial activities in the international arena concerning essentials of ideologically controlling global capitalism and reacting to emergent environmental problems depending on abuse of our common natural resources, an issue very much neglected by worldwide government policies and business practices. The findings draw attention to the value of social entrepreneuring that has been triggered by the practice of social responsibility, and almost heroic entrepreneurial assertiveness inventing imaginative change-process in poverty-traumatized global areas. Third, it relates to the positioning of social entrepreneuring as a means of widening the theoretical understanding of entrepreneurial practices in the area of the self-help movement and social environmental responsibility.

The poverty level of society is an indisputable but neglected aspect of entrepreneurship studies. Despite the growing approval of the multidisciplinary background of the field, social-related entrepreneuring[1] continues to be underemployed in entrepreneurship research (Shaw and Carter 2007). Numerous factors contribute to this state of affairs. The general tendency is that market-oriented enterprises represent the primary interest of entrepreneurship scholarship. Entrepreneurship scholars fail to recognize the role of the individual in a poverty-affected environment (Dees 1996). Even less attention is given to environmental sustainability of our business societies. It is also recognized that the field of entrepreneurship has a disproportionately quantitative focus, which makes it more complicated when studying complex fields of inquiry, such as social entrepreneurship. Moreover, social entrepreneurship in terms of research has been regarded as uninteresting contexts, and therefore unglamorous

---

[1] Entrepreneuring is defined here as an action on the part of an entrepreneur to bring about new initiatives, to create something new—such as new ideas, new ventures, or a new set of possibilities—so as to enhance people's socio-economic environment. To put it simply, entrepreneuring is what entrepreneurs do in the process of value-creating (Aggestam 2012; Rindova, Barry, and Ketchen 2009; Steyaert 2007).

and unappealing to study. Altogether, social entrepreneurs appear to have very little significance in the ever-changing world of business (Dees 1996, 1998; Austin, Stevenson, and Wei-Skillern 2006) and environmental abuse by the business and corporate world.

In this chapter it is disputed that social entrepreneurs militate against capitalistic endeavors that often are short-sighted and profit-oriented and provide portrayals of three entrepreneurial personalities, which stands out both for their capacity to move almost seamlessly between the business world and survival under poverty conditions. The other two are promoting radical changes in contemporary capitalistic society by creating awareness about industrial abuse of natural resources. They organize around assorted environmental and climate change issues, particularly those which deal with the natural environment. Their goal is to gain participation and influence in the decision-making processes of governments and businesses to take responsibilities for those destructions. In his words: "What is good for society is also good for business" (Petter Stordalen, FT.com/wealth: 42 to 43).

To illustrate this argument, the focus is on how the individual entrepreneur became a powerful force in local economic structures, continually assessing an impoverished "reality" and facilitating a climate for socio-economic and environmental change (e.g., Mair and Martí 2006; Shaw and Carter 2007). Above all, the question is what triggers social entrepreneuring and what kind of human and environmental abuse factors become incubators in the entrepreneurship initiation process. This question remains essential for entrepreneurship research and practice, holding out the promise of a more profound understanding of social entrepreneurship. The case study method is helpful for illustrating the new initiatives taken within the issues of climate changes demanding better management of resources in a new, sustainable and more long-term manner.

The study is neo-institutionalist in the sense that it draws on the insights of the radical Austrian approach to entrepreneurship—in particular, Lachmann's subjectivist perspective—to understand how the social entrepreneur creates opportunities through expectations of an imagined future and exploits opportunities to create wealth through continuous resource recombination. Conceptualizing human and environmental issues as subjective facilitates the examination of what triggers social entrepreneuring, especially when combining business with self-help movements or fighting against the abuse of our environment for the sake of economic gain.

The chapter is organized as follows. The next section provides the broad theoretical framework within which the paper is located. This is followed by a description of the case studies, which offers details on research sites, methods, and data analysis. The final section presents findings, conclusions, and implications for research and practice.

Entrepreneurship and Social Entrepreneurship

Research on social entrepreneurship has clearly benefited from previous work on entrepreneurship. The rise of social entrepreneurship as both a theoretical construct and practical approach provides a unique opportunity for the field to be enhanced. Given importance to social entrepreneurship, this study is based on conceptual insights of the Austrian economist Ludwig Lachmann who conducted a "radical re-examination of the way in which economic theory was developing … steering it in the most novel of directions" (Boehm et al. 2000), and is used here to conceptualize his challenging approach of imagination. Lachmann's original economic framework takes an interest in the intelligibility of human activities through subjective lenses and provides the overall framework that guides this chapter. Furthermore, his wide and generic view emphasizes a "unique disequilibrium perspective, which takes into account institutional context and multiple levels of analysis, [and] offers new theoretical insights into how *social* entrepreneurs create opportunities through expectations of an imagined future" (Chiles, Bluedorn, and Gupta 2007). Indeed, in some instances, such as sustainable governance of nature resources and the self-help movement,[2] using imagination actually creates an incubator for the entrepreneurship initiation process and illuminating the dynamics of social entrepreneuring.

---

[2] The self-help movement aims to change the perception of the poor by showing them how to create a new sustainable life for themselves.

The considerable insights from entrepreneurship and the neo-institutional conceptual tradition (Lachmann 1986; Scott 1995) help to understand how social entrepreneurial performance may emerge and respond to extreme poverty or the brutality of the environmental misman-agement of worldwide resources. Neo-institutionalists have focused on cog-nitive elements of individual performance based on subjectively constructed aspirations that influence and guide actions (Lachmann 1986). Drawing on these constructs together in the context of the neo-institutional tradition suggests that both *internal* (personal) and *external* (environmental) forces may prompt social entrepreneuring processes (Scott 1995).

Equal consideration is given to the entrepreneurial ability to imagine a better world for people who are involved in environmental and economic improvement processes and who are committed to creating environmen-tal sustainability and societal change worldwide. Evidence of these abil-ities, for example, may include the ability to exert authority, frame new practices and behaviors, set new agendas for organizational action, and creatively bring together unusual new ideas for the improvement of grass-roots systems. Further, they conflate into larger, international forum in the form of protest against the outrageous actions of corporations and mismanagement of societal resources for own gain, just to mention a few. Chell (2007) called capabilities of this kind "alienable" (e.g., leaders' capa-bilities, business expertise) and *"inalienable"* (e.g., tacit knowledge, other unique personal assets) resources that together comprise the intelligibil-ity[3] of social entrepreneuring.

In the same vein as Chell's view, Kwiatkowski (2004) also assigned value to embodied human capabilities (such as cognitive, emotional, and intellectual) that may benefit and distinguish the social entrepreneur over

---

[3] Social entrepreneuring takes an interest in the intelligibility of human practices. Human practice becomes intelligible through a number of factors. Studies have investigated individual psycho-social characteristics including personality traits (Chell 1985), psychodynamics (Kets de Vries 1977), personal needs and motives (e.g., McClelland 1961), socialization and societal group membership (Hagen 1962); and various combinations of socio-economic background, personal char-acteristics, education and work experience, position within the local community (Kets de Vries 1977), and the role of personal networks (e.g., Johannisson 1988; 1998).

other individuals. This form of agency requires imaginative mind-sets that have the capacity to strive "to imagine and create a better world" (Sarasvathy et al. 2003). For Sarasvathy, effectual process ends are not pre-determined but continually redefined in order to construct new "mental models" for others or to create solutions to environmental and economic problems. Dorado (2005), for instance, pointed to *projective* agency, that is, agency that is involved in imaginative thought and actions directed toward changing existing and creating novel practices and procedures.

The term "social entrepreneuring"[4] is used to refer to a number of approaches to efficiently catering for basic human needs that existing market-related business ventures and governments have failed to fulfil. More specifically, social entrepreneuring combines an emphasis on the notions of entrepreneurial creation,[5] taken basically from Lachmann (1986). It is and understood as a continuous recombinative process leads to economic progress at the societal level, intimately tied to the entre-preneur's position (Sternberg 1997; 2000). Lachmann claims that (social) entrepreneurs create plans based on their subjective, individual knowledge, visions and expectations. Expectations apply to various factors and condi-tions that focus on the unknown future that entrepreneurs have to imag-ine. For Lachmann, "entrepreneurs create ex nihilo," through what Ford (2002) called the *forward-looking process of imagining* that allows them to "think outside the box," where the box is defined largely by the limits of knowledge rooted in interpretations of the past" (Chiles, Bluedorn, and Gupta 2007). Moreover, Lachmann suggests that because various entre-preneurs interpret their past and their accumulated knowledge differently, they construct their future goals, philanthropies, and ideals subjectively.

As related earlier, an element of "entrepreneurial personality" (Chell 2007; Sternberg 2004; Sternberg et al. 2000) becomes central. Consistent with this, the focus is on the founder of the initiative (Mair and Martí 2006) whose crucial distinguishing characteristic (of social entrepreneur-ing) is cognitive ability—that is, imagining the perceived opportunities

---

[4] See Dacin, Dacin, and Matear (2010) and Shaw and Carter (2007) for various definitions of the concept within the entrepreneurship literature.

[5] Entrepreneurial creation is an issue that both Kirzner and Schumpeter neglected.

upon which action is based, action that "fits" the specific needs of the local situation and that can also catalyze socio-economic change and needs (Aggestam 2014a). Cognitive ability is defined here as a mental quality that predetermines a person's responses to and definition of a given situation (Cooley 1918), an interpretation and understanding of a shared view on humankind (Baron 2004). Drawing upon these strands of thinking is the individual entrepreneur's cognitive processing, that is, the product of individual mind and imagination that is especially significant in the social entrepreneurship movements within suffering environments and communities.

Also, the term "entrepreneuring" has a particular resonance in this study because of its dual but related dynamics: it is associated with socio-cognitive approaches focusing on "agentic" aspects of solitary entrepreneurial performance in response to environmental and poverty-related triggers and, as Chell (2007) explained it, influences entrepreneurs' actions and the ways in which they might think about or represent images of situations to themselves. This line of inquiry views the social entrepreneur as an "agent of change" who is always dependent on socio-economic circumstances but also on exclusive personalized, practical knowing, and active mental processing of situated information.

What are the challenges of social entrepreneuring? The experience of the phenomenon in practice is extremely scarce (Light 2006; Porter and Kramer 2011) and the increase in attention paid to social entrepreneurship is insignificant within entrepreneurship research. There may be reasons for this insignificance. For example, social entrepreneuring may elicit a set of affective processes in traditionally difficult business situations. Also, it may trigger emotional challenges. These challenges are often grounded in depiction, for instance, circumstances where markets are identified as failed (McMullen 2011) or a social entrepreneur's new ideas may appear in the situation where there is a considerable institutional vacuum (Austin, Stevenson, and Wei-Skillern 2006; Mair and Martí 2006) that the creation of new economic entities, philanthropy-related organizations, or start-ups are being realized without institutional support.

In addition, social entrepreneurs' actions have to reflect and accord with their individual values and intrinsic satisfaction (Aggestam 2014). This means that excitement and passion may also have to underpin their activities. In other words, social entrepreneuring can be viewed as challenging because it requires strong personal encounters to be able to handle extreme situations (at various levels of society) with empathy and balanced intelligence (Chell 2007; Sternberg 1988, 1997) and where knowledge, resources, and infrastructure are missing. Researchers largely agree that "social entrepreneuring" involves a broad set of actions of entrepreneurial agency with a social or economic mission that aims to change people, communities, and societies for the better—for example, providing creative and imaginative solutions to their most pressing social, environmental, and economic problems (Alvord, Brown, and Letts 2004; Chell 2007; Dees 1996; Mair and Martí 2006). This means that social entrepreneurs play a pivotal role in the creation of social values (Dacin, Dacin, and Matear 2010; Shaw and Carter 2007) using market-based methods to solve socio-economic and environmental problems. In opposition to the self-interest of for-profit businesses, social entrepreneurship creates new socio-economic values by using market-oriented practices specifically to sustain created values (Mair and Martí 2006) in order to bring about improvements to society.

Description of the Study

To explore the phenomenon of social entrepreneuring, I have chosen to study Hand in Hand International, an organization initiated and developed by P. Barnevik, who began his involvement by targeting the poorest segment of the population in India (see also Aggestam 2014b). The second case reveals the insides about the work of Petter and Gunhild Stordalen, originators of Stordalen's Institute, Stordalen Foundation and the GreeNudge Foundation, all of which deal with the creation of protective institutions against vagaries of the corporate world and destructions of natural resources.

I selected those cases for the purpose of understanding human and environmental factors, in particular when combining business ventures with sustainable responsibility within movements in impoverished environments. I choose to highlight these particular cases for three reasons. First, I consider as Miller et al. (2012) do, that social entrepreneuring is a particularly interesting subject for study entrepreneurial activities such as the creative, imaginative, risk-taking, achievement, confident, and independent attributes of an entrepreneur exploiting and working in a poverty-stricken environment. It illustrates how the poor and marginalized have been empowered to participate in market activities. A second, local venture creation involving small firms required the constant affirmation of their members in order to keep going. Because those small local enterprises were difficult to create (due to the lack of resources) and maintain, their founders have to keep up with education, resource management and group cooperation, just to mention a few.

Third, there are two diverse structures of entrepreneurial activities in those two cases; the first one is concerned with the umbrella organization created by Percy Barnevik, a high-profile Swedish entrepreneur, and the second case is concerned with organizations building focused on developing worldwide awareness of environmental abuses of natural resources created by Gunhild and Petter Stordalen. Moreover, the Hand in Hand structure has been effective in enabling the continued building and existence of small firms, and Barnevik's model has been replicated in many developing countries. Also, Petter Stordalen is an unusual example of an anti-capitalist billionaire who is a committed environmental activist but also incorporates his and Gunhild's ideas into their businesses. For example, their company GreeNudge puts considerable pressure on international communities to create protective institutions against the vagaries of the market.

Above all, these cases provide a unique opportunity to understand social entrepreneurship and its impact on society while implementing their imaginative ideas at various levels of societies. Equally central to social entrepreneurship is the notion that, as Petter Stordalen says: "If we don't take responsibility when we run our businesses our planet will go straight to hell."

Methodology

The neo-institutional perspective has implication for the methodologies in this study. Essentially, my intention was not to chronologically document lives or activities of social entrepreneurs. I was more fascinated by understanding the meaning their visions, ideas, actions, and events held for them. Social entrepreneurs have shown extraordinary committed personalities characterized by constant affirmation and faith in their activities/doings focused on the beneficiaries and receivers for continued existence.

This focus on the understanding of the shared meaning of the social entrepreneurial activities, beneficiaries' accounts, and rapidly transforming natural environment provided limelight and enhanced the methodological stand of the study.

The neo-institutional perspective also has consequence for the methods used. The methodology was qualitative and essentially case study based. The data collection technique was based on primary and secondary data, retrieving documents directly from Hand in Hand International from 2012; media research such as the *Guardian* and *Washington Post* newspapers; Percy Barnevik's (2012) autobiography, *Jag Vill Förändra Världen* [*I Want to Change the World*], the book on Barnevik by Haag and Petersson (1999); and the book on the "new global leaders" by Kets de Vries and Florent-Treacy (1999). Information about Gunhild and Petter Stordalen was retrieved from the media, in particular from the *Financial Times* where I first discovered their existence. My intention has been not to follow worldwide developments chronologically but rather to understand the role and triggers of both entrepreneurs and also how the various activities unfolded. To understand the entrepreneurial mind-set, the biographies have been very helpful. The analysis of documents retrieved from the Internet covered a period of one year. Finally, I analyzed all documents and material for common themes relevant to the special interest in this chapter. My documents analysis was guided by a meaning-centered perspective (Taylor and Bogdan 1984) rather than focusing entirely on reporting statistics. However, I included some illustrative statistics to provide an accurate picture of the field.

1. Intrinsic Case Study

This case study did not set out to test hypotheses or attempt to confirm *a priori* theories about the social entrepreneurship processes within the context of the self-help movement. In selecting these cases, the aim was to generate novel insights and understand the dynamics of a single setting, upon which I developed my analysis. However, a single setting does not usually offer grounds for generalization to other settings, and this may constitute a limitation of the study. These case studies were also guided by Czarniawska-Joerges' (1996) notion that theory enriches practice, but only by "virtue of reflection," and they are not presenting speculatively constructed models in advance. Grounded in such perspectives, these cases are best characterized as an "intrinsic case study" (Stake 1994) that provided insights and allowed reflective understanding of the activities taken by social entrepreneurs.

In this research, a case study approach has been used following Stake (1994). This means that the analysis uses what Chia (1996) identifies as an "ontology of becoming" (as contrary to an ontology of being). The premise was that the case is not a method but an object to be studied (Stake 1994). I was attracted to Stake's approach because he was interested in studying how individual members of our society came to make sense of the social and economic environment worldwide. Stake (1994) distinguished *intrinsic*,[6] *instrumental*, and *collective* cases. Intrinsic cases, which were the focus of this study, are chosen because they enable the researcher to discover and understand the phenomena of interest. The primary purpose of such a study of a case is discovery, not theory-testing. The approach also allowed for a widening of the theoretical explanation of entrepreneurial practices that bring about economic and environmental change, development of societies, and entrepreneurship.

2. Markers of Difference: Percy Barnevik and Petter and Gunhild Stordalen

This section presents two unique social entrepreneurs. Key to these insights offered is the globalized capitalism that constituted the context where they lived their lives as business people.

Percy Barnevik represents and provides an example of philanthrocapitalism, understood here as a regenerative model of capitalism in which resources are returned to society. It can be distinguished by operations using business principles. Born in 1941, a Swedish business chief executive, chairman of multinational and

---

[6] Intrinsic cases are exemplified by: *Akenfield* (Blythe 1955/1969); *Argonauts of the Western Pacific* (Malinowski 1922/1984); *God's Choice* (Peshkin 1986).

global corporations such as ABB (1988–2002), Investor AB, General Motors, AstraZeneca, Sandvik, Asea and many other worldwide conglomerates, Barnevik turned to philanthropy after a high-profile corporate career. Broadly, he intended to lift millions of people, mainly in non-industrialized countries, out of the world's deepest poverty and has channeled large amounts of his own private funds into welfare schemes. He is the only social entrepreneur who is actively practicing and applying entrepreneurship using business principles in projects focused on eliminating poverty in several poverty-stricken countries.

Petter Stordalen owns the largest hotel chain in Scandinavia, Nordic Choice Hotels, with 170 high-end hotels in many countries, employs 10,000 people, and controls 11 well-established brands. His career started at age 10 within the strawberry business, helping his father's grocery store to flourish. The next step in his business career was the foundation of Steen and Strom Invest, one of Norway's biggest real estate companies. His interests centered on not only issues related to business world but also the environment. He has been a dedicated environmentalist, as became evident to the world when in 2002 he chained himself to the UK's Sellafield nuclear reprocessing plant in protest of handling nuclear waste. In 2007, he was charged with trespassing after entering a top-secret area on Malmøykalven, an island close to Oslo, to protest at the dumping of toxic mud. His background is one of social and economic privilege, and his concerns about our environment originated from his practical concerns. He says: "It started when we started to look at energy? We wanted to save energy because we wanted to save money" (FT/Wealth: 44 to 45). At that point he was not aware of the role that the natural environment was playing; such thoughts only occur to him later. He describes himself as a "techno-optimist" and sees his responsibility to promote new technology as catalyst for change. His interest in electricity issues led him to invest in Think Global, an Oslo-based electric car company, which ended in what he called "disaster" or financial collapse. His green outlook is grounded in the view that people are at risk if they fail to respect the planet's natural limits. His view is that climate change is being ignored and that we are embarking on a battle between capitalism and free market fundamentalism on the one hand, and an overheated planet on the other. For the moment, capitalism is winning. It wins every time, for example, when corporation and big business talk about economic growth and whenever this leads to the breaking of emissions commitments already made. The spiral of market fundamentalists' action is outside public control. The catastrophic results of this muddying and procrastination are now undeniable.

"Hand in Hand International" and Percy Barnevik

1. Initiation Process

Hand in Hand was founded by two Swedish teachers, Gunnel and Ole Blomquist, in 1988 as a small project to help free small children (from four years old) from industrial slavery. These children were basically sold or given away by their parents who had borrowed money from local milling/weaving companies that they were unable to repay. The Blomquists were traumatized by situations characterized as poverty, illiteracy, and hunger, and started raising funds to enable to free the children from the oppressive conditions in which they lived. They were committed to making a difference, but resources were very limited. At first their goal was to feed the hungry children after the long hours they spent working. The next step was to find premises in which to start schools, and to provide school uniforms, school buses, and education in English. This was the beginning of the initiative to buy the children back from the industries for which they worked. They wanted to build a better and sustainable future for children freed from industrial slavery as well as for those still enslaved. A third development within the project was an initiative to build simple housing in villages. They networked widely to find the resources and they actively sought outside help. At this point, their first contact with Percy Barnevik occurred. He visited their small site in 2003 and started to be involved in the project. This involvement was initiated by the expansion of schools and was focused mainly on the education and economic empowerment of women. Generally, men were untrustworthy and almost never repaid their loans, offering various excuses, and also lacked a sense of responsibility for their obligations. Women paid back 99.7 percent of their loans and were willing to learn, work hard, and take responsibility. The aim has been to educate them to start their own ventures in the future.

Hand in Hand International is an exclusive model of microfinance. It targets the very poorest level of society (living on less than a dollar a day), individual women or groups who have never had business-related opportunities in the globalized capitalist economy or run any form of cash-related venture.

Loans averaging $125 were given predominantly to women running or starting new ventures. The model is unique in its own way because it is based on a projection of success and prosperity. Consequently, in order to borrow more money, the women went through a period of comprehensive training. The women need to show that they understand their own self-interest and their involvement in their small ventures. Percy Barnevik says: "We teach 75 000 women a year to read, write, and do basic math in 150 days." This is followed by training in entrepreneurship, finance, and basic operations in a variety of ventures such as baking, sewing, or making jute bags. That takes three to four months. After this extensive training, a cash injection may be available and this has to be invested directly in the small business created. The cash borrowed is closely monitored so that it is spent on creating ventures and not on consumption. The aim is to develop skills for self-employment and provide income needed to support the family or individual. The model also has extensive social requirements apart from providing microloans.

Child labor has been a critical problem in India. Realizing that child labor could not be eliminated without raising the living standards of parents, a five-pronged strategy is followed: education, health, dissemination of government schemes for the underprivileged, incorporating microfinance, and awareness of the importance of a clean environment and personal hygiene.

It demands that the health situation is improved, that children are forced out of work and into schools (some 30,000 pupils have been freed) and that villages are basically cleaned. These factors are connected and create a self-sustaining way of life. Hand in Hand may, for example, help to provide villages with new school teachers, but the villagers have to pay the teachers' wages out of their own resources. Hand in Hand does not allow the situation of "dependency" on outside help, and the aim is to create prosperity based on villagers' understanding of the situation.

In 2012, Hand in Hand provided help to 771,000 Indian women, who have created 810,000 small business ventures and 5,500 medium-sized companies. The number is growing by 400 a day. The microfinance model has also been expanded to South Africa, China, Brazil, and Afghanistan. According to Barnevik, the goal is to help a billion people who live on less than a dollar a day. He posits that creating a job costs approximately $200 in non-industrial countries and that the industrial world is inefficiently spending $110 billion a year on aid. Applying this model may potentially have a huge impact on the development of the poorest and lessen various economic and social tensions.

2. The Concept of Success

The experience of Hand in Hand International is that women repay 99.7 percent of their loans. The loans make it possible for women to create financial independence by setting up small ventures. As the system develops, a self-help movement starts. Percy Barnevik donated $17 million of his own money to Hand in Hand International. He says that "the most important thing here is our knowledge, ability and passion." Those are the factors that help to create incubators in the entrepreneurship initiation processes. Engaging in a process of continuous learning, initiation, and practical adaptation, he is very efficient at soliciting support from other donors. Importantly, he adds:

... everything is quantified. All the way down to the bottom you have targets and follow-up, like in a super-efficient company. Productivity and quality everywhere. Therefore, I get so irritated when I read these big bilateral aid organizations saying it's very difficult to measure. Not at all. It's like hospitals and schools and everything. They say: These are people, you can't measure people. I say: Bullshit, you can measure it. (*Guardian*, 22 January 2008)

Percy's formula relies heavily on volunteers: 50,000 of them, in addition to the 2,600 people he currently employs. He gets deeply involved in anticipating the needs of people for whom no one really cared before. He then provides a business survival model that insists on extensive training for borrowers. This training not only provides rules for their ventures but also redefines their life. "Everything I learned as a CEO applies in this world as well," he says (*Washington Post*, December 23, 2008). The idea is to listen closely to women and society and to their basic problems. But the vision is personal. Percy Barnevik, of course, is one member of a large team at Hand and Hand International, and he makes decisions and choices. Mostly he relies on tenacity, trust, and his own judgment and looks for the multiplier factor of excellence on a small scale. There is a tight connection between his personality as a social entrepreneur and what he is creating. In the poverty universe, Percy Barnevik inspires people to be innovative, engaged, and active. He is genuinely interested in articulating his socio-economic vision of improvement, which he passionately pursues. His critical set of ingredients for success is enthusiasm, creativity, and passion (interview on Swedish Radio, October 15, 2011). Above all, the empowerment of women who were in the most abject poverty demonstrates the imaginative and original way in which the process was conducted. This has been done without regard to local traditions. Percy Barnevik has been a pioneer in locating opportunities for women that prove beneficial. The definition of the situation was instrumental in dictating Barnevik's new initiatives, imagination, and passion for work. He underscores that for him the most serious gift—arguably the only serious one—is our knowledge, abilities, and passions. According to Vaishna Roy, communications officer of Hand in Hand International:

> This place is run like a corporate. Percy keeps telling us not to measure ourselves against other NGOs but with companies. We have regular board meetings, prepare annual reports and have fixed targets. Percy reads the reports and distributes them to the other potential donors abroad. He is an impressive figure. He used to joke about how he bathed using a small bucket and a mug and about all the children in the village following him when he went on his morning jogs.

Another employee, N. Sivakumar, who first met him in 2007, says:

> He is very motivating and also precise. If somebody gives an idea,
> he refuses to accept a vague outline and insists that it is action-
> oriented. He also comes up with new ideas. Percy is constantly
> asking us, how many lives have you touched?

By the end of 2012, Hand in Hand International had helped set up
1, 244,260 sustainable jobs, 771,000 mobilized and trained women, and
810,000 small enterprises. Another initiative involving Barnevik was started
in 1998 in Kancheepuram by a group of Swedish women who wanted to
stop the child laborers working in mills there. Barnevik entered the stage in
2002, changing it into a not-for-profit enterprise across 18 districts, in four
states in the country. The same model has been adopted in South Africa,
Afghanistan, and Brazil. The model of venture creation in Central and
North India was shaped by speed, low costs, scale, and transparency.

The Stordalens

Petter Stordalen. Petter Stordalen owns one of the biggest hotel chains
in Scandinavia and his net worth is $1.61 billion. He is the owner and
CEO of Home Invest, Chairman of the board of Nordic Choice Hotels
and Home Properties, and board member of Home Capital. He is also a
partner in the Stordalen Foundation, which supports the European Climate Foundation and is one of the eight major contributors. His personal
philosophy based on corporate responsibility at Nordic Choice Hotels
led to the removal of pornography from pay TV in its bedrooms, and in
2007 the company became the world's first smoke-free hotel chain. In
2008, every hotel was certified in accordance with the ISO 14001 stan-
dard. The hotel restaurants provide meat but guests are recommended
healthy eating choices. The company also works with Rainforest Foundation Norway and helped preserve 53,600 hectares of tropical rainforest in
2012. The same year, Nordic Choice Hotels won the Grand Travel Award
for Best Work Place for the fourth year in a row.

He is a committed environmentalist and has been aware of how
corporate interests have systematically exploited our common natural

resources leading to environmental disaster. All such natural disasters produce new irony-laden accounts of a climate increasingly inhospitable to the very businesses, corporations, or industries that are mostly responsible for them in the first place. He also takes action himself. For instance, in 2002, he chained himself to the UK's Shellafield nuclear reprocessing plant in protest of governmental approval of treating nuclear waste. In 2010 he married Gunhild, who holds a PhD in medicine and who inspired Petter Stordalen to undertake philanthropic pursuits, which resulted in founding Stordalen Institute with the goal of promoting social and environmental responsibility. A combination of Petter's ideals and money and Gunhild's knowledgeable beliefs are aiming to make capitalism more human-friendly. They are pioneers in the area of fighting abuses of our natural resources by capitalistic companies and corporation and say if we do not act now to protect our environment, the world "will go to hell." Both Gunhild and Petter work together in various companies and associations, and their motto is "eat healthy and make an effort to develop the world's sustainable food production." For example, Choice Hotels provide 70 percent organic food. The main big issues of our time, is how we can feed nine billion people with healthy food without totally destroying our planet.

They are constantly developing new ideas in order to find common ground for people's health, sustainability, and acting for synergies that may influence industries, politicians, and scholarly research. Their aim is to work more closely with capitalist forces in industry in order to integrate sustainability with enterprise "DNA" in order to identify sustainable research opportunities and to quicken the pace of change processes.

Gunhild Stordalen. Gunhild Storedalen is cofounder and chair of Stordalen Foundation and CEO of GreeNudge, director of the board of Nordic Choice Hospitality Group, Eco, Zero, and European Climate Foundation. She is a founder member and the chairman of the board of the Stordalen Foundation. She is a medical doctor from the University of Oslo and holds a PhD in pathology/orthopedics, and a member of the Norwegian Medical Association's committee for human rights, climate change, and global health. She is totally dedicated to climate- and health-related issues and strongly supports sustainability initiatives.

1. Stordalen Foundation

The Stordalen Foundation was co-founded with Gunhild Stordalen. Their actions could be primarily explained as: fighting for the world and give the planet the chance to survive. They understand climate change as essentially a battle between capitalism and the planet—and for the moment capitalism is undeniably winning. It wins every time a corporation talks about economic growth and uses it as an excuse for breaking emissions commitments already made. Enterprises and corporate interests have systematically exploited our natural resources enriching financially only a small group of people. They did so by lifting regulation, cutting social spending, and forcing large-scale privatizations of public sphere, among the other actions. For example, communal forests around the world are being turned into corporate hands building legally new business formation: "tree farms." Those tree farms refer to ways in which the industrial world and big corporation preserved their beneficial financial interests throughout international exchange system called "carbon credits." In other words, the global community has been drained of natural resources by industry and big corporations who enacted environments through "carbon credits" exchange system, called sometimes as a very lucrative scam. Accumulation of natural disasters produces new irony-laden records of increasingly inhospitable climate pointing at the very business and corporate world most responsible for its cause and warming. That is one way to see how market fundamentalism helps overheat the planet.

The Stordalen Foundation also supports other initiatives that promote animal welfare such as Blue Cross in UK and Dyrebeskyttelsen Kongsberg in Denmark. Other projects include Water for Life, which has helped to build wells and to improve sanitary conditions for school children in Malawi, Nepal, and Madagascar. Also Nordic Choice and UNICEF started a three-year project, Free to Grow, in order to help children grow up free from violence and violations of their rights.

Through Nordic Choice Hotels, the Stordalen Foundation finances European Climate Foundation (ECF), as one of eight largest sponsors. The ECF was created in 2008 to promote climate and energy policies that greatly reduce Europe's greenhouse gas emissions and help Europe play an even stronger international leadership role in mitigating climate change. The organization drives its own projects but also finances and helps set policy for a number of climate related organizations in Europe. Gunhild Stordalen has served on the supervisory board since 2010.

2. GreeNudge and Gunhild and Petter Stordalen

   GreeNudge (www.greenudge.no), financially supported by the Stordalen Foundation, aims at promoting and financing projects related to climate measurement and behavioral research. Established in 2011 in Oslo, Norway, GreeNudge is a not-for-profit organization that is working together with various intergovernmental bodies entrusted with disaster prevention, research institutions, organizations, and businesses to create new knowledge on cost-effective measures that incentivize climate-friendly behavior. Fighting for our collective chances of survival, they hope that those new findings and new instruments can be implemented on a larger scale and thereby reduce emissions significantly. The organization also aims to understand how the global food system contributes to greenhouse gas emissions, providing for research and promoting ways to reducing them. Broadly, it strongly promotes and enables sustainable choices in everyday life to create emission-free solutions and green growth. It is also part of Danish Nugin Network. GreeNudge is led by Gunhild Stordalen and an operational council that consists of a multidisciplinary team that includes climate researchers, consumer researchers, and a deputy director. The organization runs its own projects but also supports a number of climate change-related endeavors, thereby strengthening feelings of solidarity and eliciting considerable public support.

3. EAT: Science, politics and business sharing food for thought

   In 2013, The Stordalen Foundation, in cooperation with the Stockholm Resilience Centre, started EAT—an international consortium, a platform for world leading universities, research centers, governments, philanthropic foundations, non-government actors and organizations, and companies, in which all share the common understanding that it is essential to collectively address issues of food, health, and sustainability primarily framed to save the planet (www.eatforum.org/partner/stordalen-foundation). This requires more interdisciplinary knowledge of the interconnections between food and agriculture, health and nutrition, environmental sustainability, and socio-economic factors. Scientific research is at the heart of the EAT Initiative, and the flagship of its structural design is a network of world-leading universities and research institutions, with the common objective of advancing knowledge and identifying synergistic solutions within the nexus of food, health, and sustainability.

Findings and Interpretation

This section presents a broader conception of social entrepreneuring based on discussion of the case study data and findings from a neo-institutionalist standpoint. As indicated previously, my intent was to inform entrepreneurship scholars and practitioners on those aspects of social entrepreneuring not captured by other perspectives. In highlighting the progressively developed success of social entrepreneur Percy Barnevik and how he pursued his mission in the self-help movement model he created, this chapter emphasizes the business aspects of social entrepreneuring, in particular illustrating how his work has been carried out successfully. Thus far, it is also evident that Gunhild and Petter Stordalen's radical activities are illustrative for taking responsibilities for sustainable resource management both in home country and internationally. This process of influencing the business context involved providing clear examples of for-profit companies that have been enhanced by sustainable management of resources and also focused environmental responsibility. Following this path, this study also offers a certain theoretical framework for successful venture creation and practical articulation of sustainable environmental responsibilities within the social entrepreneuring approach.

An analysis of the Hand in Hand organization suggests that successful social entrepreneuring was built around the powerful presence and experience of Percy Barnevik who promoted autonomy, inclusion, trust, imagination, excitement, and passion to enhance the self-worth of local individuals in order to eradicate poverty in all its forms. Therefore, this study implies that unspecified and non-concrete goals and purposes for survival in impoverished areas are ineffective if not linked to the personal experience of the individual social entrepreneur.

The case of Percy Barnevik exclusively illustrated the process of creating business values by providing solutions to social problems. His undertakings and organizing drive aimed to impose a new order and new patterns of life in villages and have been based on his personal analytical and practical capabilities, as clearly demonstrated. More specifically, his predispositions in this case study were partly personal (internal), and partly environmental (external), stimulated by conditions of extreme poverty and willingness to help others better themselves. From this, it also follows that social entrepreneuring—or what Sternberg (1997) termed "balanced intelligence"—is at the crux of venture creation and establishment. Such subjective knowledge suggests that successful venture creation often rests on the individual's ability to be analytical, creative, and practical. (See Table 1.1 for cases that are indicative and illustrative of how they were carried on in various contexts and how new meaningful realities have been created in poverty regions.)

Table 1.1 Examples of the new entrepreneur

New entrepreneurs	Quotation from H & H international cases
Nadera, North Afghanistan	She did not believe that she had the skills to run her own business. Today she has a business plan and runs her own poultry farm with help from her mother.
Christine, Machakos, Kenya	For the first time she began saving money each week and learning the business skills she needed to start her own business. She is 67 years old and started her own business making and selling baskets and rope.
Usha, India	To begin with she set up a tailoring business. This was so successful she took out another loan and bought a taxi or "share auto." Today she runs two businesses, earns 6000 INR per month (US$120) and employs her brother as the taxi driver.
Thandazile, Swaziland	She learned financial discipline and received business training before taking a loan to establish a piggery, supplying local restaurants and supermarkets. Today her business has an annual turnover of US$3500.
Cathrine, Eastern Africa	Inspired by business training, she also has a business plan. She has taken a loan so that she can build up her farming business to include chickens, a goat, and a dairy cow.

Source: Case studies from Hand in Hand International projects in various countries.

By highlighting these newly created successful small businesses and turning attention to learning and believing in its own business and survival capacity, we can see the emergence of meaningful realities for those women whose previous shared reality was one of poverty and starvation. They have been able to transform their own context and socio-economic status.

In highlighting the success of Barnevik and also the Stordalens, I am not implying that their strategies were perfect or their activities were not beset by problems and political contradictions. Rather, their actions demonstrated the enormous complexity of the processes they were involved in and that their accomplishment was based on their imagination, past business experiences, and considerable corporate practices. These were combined with what Chell (2007) called "alienable" resources, such as leadership, business planning expertise, and other performative skills that build on and ensure the success of their activities. In both cases, the nature of the social entrepreneur is conceived as a product based not only on his business background but also on the values of his national heritage.

Lachmann's notion of individual knowledge, experience, and expectations being the critical component of a social entrepreneur's ability to engage in the venture creation process seems to hold true. My findings demonstrate that both Stordalen's and Barnevik's creative actions seemed to be about what Ford (2002) called the *forward-looking process* of *imagining* that allowed them to stretch out over time and space, and also provided the signaling mechanism allowing them to initiate new environmentally friendly and developmental projects. Both entrepreneurs provided hard financial resources as well as a softer, personal support mechanism through their links. Characteristics and consistent outcomes were also ascribed to their personalities that have been shaped by the credibility of business experiences and incubation of their ideas. Stordalen's case demonstrated also the way he has been building his own credibility within local business milieu by providing and sustaining eco-friendly rules. The important goal for him was the maintenance of his credibility as demonstrated by the degree of his involvement in the projects. Both entrepreneurs have been aggressive in framing and applying their experiences at the local and international level of activity. This persistence also helped to build influence in Europe.

My findings also provide evidence in support of entrepreneurs' instantiating social entrepreneuring through their cognitive abilities, which are a combination of analytical, creative, and practical skills useful in the process of imagining the future. As these cases show, Barnevik and Stordalen cognized the women differently and, based on these cognitive abilities, make decisions to support and promote their ideas. The study shows that in Barnevik's case, only women have been capable of sustaining their business successfully. Gunhild Stordalen becomes most exemplary and significant Scandinavian women who not only inspired but also created organization important for survival of our planet.

Another factor that appears to be highly personalized was the empathetic awareness of the situation, alongside cognition of facts that problematized the very nature of the abused natural resources and poverty-stricken environments. The data shows that fundamental capitalist-driven resource abuse by the business world and their controversial tactics lucks strong opponents. They proceed with their damaging actions as they wish to. On the other hand, the poverty-stricken environments did not have the economic power to create an existence of its own. Rather, it suggests that successful environmentally friendly progress-building is fostered around forward-looking personal imagination, expertise, and balanced intelligence. In short, the evidence demonstrates that the cognitive-related attributes of entrepreneurs represent one of the major resources for social entrepreneuring. Furthermore, by using these attributes, the process of social entrepreneuring has been initiated, enhanced, and solidified.

Conclusions

The aim of this chapter was to provide a solid foundation on which conceptualization of social entrepreneurial processes can proceed. To achieve this, the chapter provided a brief introduction to Lachmann's ideas, which run counter to the current mainstream entrepreneurship paradigm based on Schumpeter and Kirzner (e.g., Shane and Venkataraman 2000). Lachmann shed unique light on entrepreneurial creation, issues that both Schumpeter and Kirzner neglected, and also opened up new ways of thinking about entrepreneurial exploitation of opportunities as a continuous recombinative process (Chiles, Bluedorn, and Gupta 2007).

Empirically based theorizing offers a broad challenge to mainstream entrepreneurship studies by foregrounding the emergence of creative entrepreneurial practice, which comprises personal roles and dynamics. Moreover, meaningful actions of social entrepreneurs are more difficult to build, maintain, and sustain than are business enterprises mainly because they have to possess highly personalized empathetic awareness, alongside an awareness of the situation and common sense. Also that include a forward-looking vision to be able to develop socially responsible alliances.

Examining social entrepreneuring processes allowed the identification of the nature of the social entrepreneur as highly personalized and emphasizes the individual contribution to socially responsible actions toward business and survival of our societies and also to the self-help movement in the developing world. That is, social entrepreneurship can operate essentially as a creative act that uses forward-looking inventive imagination and capital resources to empower disadvantaged people and encourage them to take control of their lives. It is applicable when a powerful and high-status entrepreneur endorses these practices—an emphasis that is important for widening our theoretical and practical understanding of activities that are labeled "social entrepreneuring."

The analysis suggests that an individual's capabilities are important for the success of social entrepreneuring. Accordingly, the findings reveal that the situations in which social entrepreneurs are not fulfilling their promises and obligations depend on their lack of competence and personal attributes. Stordalen and Barnevik are an illustration of the opposite. They have the capabilities to evaluate progress by how well they and the others in the projects prosper and improve the situation. Both cases draw heavily on their private achievements in business and the pivotal role given to triggers, which facilitated their actions.

Findings and analysis revealed that *women* are the instrumental driving force for economic growth in a poverty-stricken society. It was evident that only women were able to work with Percy Barnevik to make their projects succeed. Women initiated new ventures and have had a significant impact on their home economy and on ending extreme poverty in their localities. The case strongly indicated that women's venture creation within Hand in Hand International may also be positioned as a unique kind of opportunity for developing society not only economically but also sustainably. That said, the research results discussed here suggest the need for further work to examine the performance and growth of women's businesses within the self-help movement. Entrepreneurship scholars could also enrich the approaches of both Lachmann and Sternberg by building connections between them and studying women in this successful project. Another reason to extensively study this group of women is the lack of studies and models that can be used to explain and disseminate the results worldwide.

To conclude, my analysis also demonstrates that social entrepreneuring is a process of creating *conditions* for both environmental and developmental movements. This is a critical part that requires greater depth of understanding to make a difference in the business and corporate skullduggery and social sphere.

Another interesting issue within social entrepreneurship is philanthropy that sees creation of sustainable businesses as a primary practice to provide a holistic view of problems and solutions in the process of wealth creation (Edwards 2008). Philanthropy accentuates the interpretation of social issues (Miller et al. 2012) as the root of entrepreneurial action. In functional terms it can be distinguished from more conventional approaches such as non-governmental and other nonprofit aid organizations as it reinforces and applies entrepreneurial capabilities and score-keeping to our most persistent challenges in order to create responsible and sustainable wealth. This approach primarily challenges various socio-economic and environmental issues such as poverty, homelessness, child slavery, environmental abuse of resources by corporate business spheres, and other societal problems (Bishop and Green 2009). When it comes to understanding basic grounds of social entrepreneurship, the commitment to economic and social values (Austin, Stevenson, and Wei-Skillern 2006) used by market-based organizational forms become important for sustainability and survival (Mair and Martí 2006; Hartigan 2006) of our planet. This endogenic stance of social entrepreneurships harmonizes with Weber's (1968) notion of understanding the situation (*verstehen*) that helps scholars encounter developmental challenges by paying attention to meaningful realities (Chell 2000; Dempsey and Sanders 2010) and actions of social entrepreneurs. Consequently, defining meaningful realities precedes the actual identification of socio-economic problems by defining the situation (Cooley 1918), a process where social entrepreneurs through creative, analytical, and practical thinking (Sternberg 1997) imagine future solutions (Lachmann 1986). Again it was apparent in both cases that the definition of the situation was instrumental and was a process element in shaping the eventual choice of tactics and market-based methods toward imagined solutions. It is in this way that understanding of social entrepreneuring ideas can be helpful.

Implications: The Future for Social Entrepreneuring in Entrepreneurship Research

While the social entrepreneurship approach within entrepreneurship research has not substantially increased in popularity over the years, the concept itself is not new and has been used in the past by various social scientists. Although its use has intensified slightly, due to its founding personalities, "business angels," leaders of big corporations, global companies, and other "visible" actors, much entrepreneurship research has been overlooked. A perspective that has not been fully explored, for the reasons mentioned earlier, is that of the cross-disciplinary approach of, for example, entrepreneurial action. However, as highlighted in the previous discussion, social entrepreneurship involvement can also be problematic. Yet, it is through social entrepreneurship that successful entrepreneurial action can convert "lack of resources" into a "small venture" and "job creation" into a "sustainable environment" for the poverty-stricken population. Despite some empirical and theoretical development (e.g., Grant and Berry 2011; Miller et al. 2012), there is a need for further understanding of particular social issues that may involve social entrepreneurs, the embeddedness of the process they are involved in, and the impact of socio-economic mechanisms on the process of creation of meaningful realities for the poor.

While this case study has demonstrated that social entrepreneuring is a process creating *conditions* for a successful self-help movement, further research is needed to generate findings in other contexts. I have also argued that by conceptualizing social entrepreneuring we can understand better what triggers social entrepreneuring and what kind of human and contextual factors become incubators in the entrepreneurship process. The crucial element of future research on social entrepreneurship is a cross-disciplinary agenda. Such a cross-disciplinary agenda could be useful in studying, for example, the entrepreneurial potential of women in poverty-stricken environments, the view of investors within the world of extreme poverty, or documenting how social entrepreneurs move from conception to implementation. Implications for practitioners lie in highlighting the importance of balanced intelligence combined with personal imagination when working within extreme poverty situations.

References

Aggestam, M. 2014a. "Conceptualizing Entrepreneurial Capital in the Context of Institutional Change." *International Entrepreneurship and Management Journal* 10, no. 1, pp. 165–186.

Aggestam, M. 2014b. "Social Entrepreneuring: The Case of Swedish Philanthrocapitalism." In *Entrepreneurship, People and Organisations: Frontiers in European Entrepreneurship Research,* eds. R. Blackburn, F. Delmar, A. Fayolle and F. Welter. Cheltenham: Edward Elgar.

Alvord, S., L. Brown, and C. Letts. 2004. "Social Entrepreneurship and Societal Transformation." *Journal of Applied Behavioural Science* 40, no. 3, pp. 260–282.

Austin, J., H. Stevenson, and J. Wei-Skillern. 2006. "Social and Commercial Entrepreneurship: Same, Different, or Both?" *Entrepreneurship Theory and Practice* 30, no. 1, pp. 1–22.

Barnevik, P. 2012. *Jag Vill Förändra Världen* [I Want to Change the World]. Stockholm: Månpocket.

Baron, R. 2004. "Opportunity Recognition: A Cognitive Perspective." *Academy of Management Proceedings*, pp. A1–A6.

Bishop, M. 2010. *Philanthrocapitalism: How Giving Can Save The World*. New York: Bloomsburg Press.

Boehm, S., I. Kirzner R. Koppl, D. Lavoie, and P. Lewin. 2000. "Remembrance and Appreciation Roundtable—Professor Ludvig M. Lachmann." *American Journal of Economics and Sociology* 59, no. 3, pp. 367–417.

Chell, E. 2000. "Toward Researching the 'Opportunistic Entrepreneur': A Social Constructionist Approach and Research Agenda." *European Journal of Work and Organizational Psychology* 9, no. 1, pp. 63–80.

Chell, E. 2007. "Social Enterprise and Entrepreneurship: Toward a Convergent Theory of the Entrepreneurial Process." *International Small Business Journal* 25, no. 1, pp. 5–26.

Chiles, T., A. Bluedorn, and V Gupta. 2007. "Beyond Creative Destruction and Entrepreneurial Discovery: A Radical Austrian Approach to Entrepreneurship." *Organization Studies* 28, no. 4, pp. 467–493.

Chia, R. 1996. *Organizational Analysis as Deconstructive Practice.* Berlin, Germany and New York: De Gruyter.

Cooley, C.H. 1918. *Social Process.* New York: Scribner.

Czarniawska-Joerges, B. 1996. *A City Reframed: Managing Warsaw in the 1990s.* Sweden: GRI, Gothenburg University.

Dacin, P., T. Dacin, and M. Matear. 2010. "Social Entrepreneurship: Why We Don't Need a New Theory and How We Move Forward from Here." *Academy of Management Perspectives* 24, no. 3, pp. 37–57.

Dees, J. 1998. *The Meaning of Social Entrepreneurship* available at www.redalmarza. com/ing/pdf.

Dempsey, S. and M. Sanders. 2010. "Meaningful Work? Nonprofit Marketization and Work/Life Imbalance in Popular Autobiographies of Social Entrepreneurship" *Organization* 17, no. 4, pp. 437–459.

Dorado, S. 2005. "Institutional Entrepreneurship, Partaking, and Convening." *Organization Studies* 26, no. 3, pp. 385–414.

Edwards, M. 2008. 'Philanthrocapitalism and its Limits." *International Journal of Not for Profit Law* 10, no. 2, pp. 22–29.

Ford, C. 2002. "The Futurity of Decisions as a Facilitator of Organizational Creativity and Change." *Journal of Organizational Change Management* 15, no. 6, pp. 635–646.

Grant, A. and J. Berry. 2011. "The Necessity of Others is the Mother of Invention: Intrinsic and Prosocial Motivations, Perspective Taking and Creativity." *Academy of Management Journal* 54, no. 1, pp. 73–96.

Haag, M. and B. Petersson 1999. *Percy Barnevik: Makten, Myten, Människan* [Percy Barnevik: The Power, the Myth, and the Person]. Stockholm: Ekerlids.

Hartigan, P. 2006. "It's About People, not Profits." *Business Strategy Review* 17, no. 4, pp. 42–45.

Johannisson, B. 1988. "Business Formation—A Network Approach." *Scandinavian Journal of Management* 4, nos. 3–4, pp. 83–99.

Kets de Vries, M., and E. Florent-Treacy. 1999. *The New Global Leaders: Richard Branson, Percy Barnevik, David Simon and Remaking of the International Business.* San Francisco: Jossey-Bass.

Kwiatkowski, S. 2004. "Social and Intellectual Dimensions of Entrepreneurship." *Higher Education in Europe* 29, no. 2, pp. 205–220.

Lachmann, L. 1986. *The Market as an Economic Process.* Oxford: Basil Blackwell.

Light, P. 2006. "Searching for Social Entrepreneurs." In *Research on Social Entrepreneurship: Understanding and Contributing to an Emerging Field,* ed. R. Mosher-Williams, pp. 89–104. Indianapolis: Association for Research on Nonprofits Organizations and Voluntary Action.

Mair, J., and I. Martí. 2006. "Social Entrepreneurship Research: A Source of Explanation, Prediction and Delight." *Journal of World Business* 41, no. 1, pp. 36–44.

McClelland, D. 1961. *The Achieving Society.* New York: Van Nostrand.

McMullen, J. S. (2011), Delineating the Domain of Development Entrepreneurship: A Market-Based Approach to Facilitating Inclusive Economic Growth. *Entrepreneurship Theory and Practice,* no. 35, pp. 185–193.

Miller, T., M. Grimes, J. McMullen, and T. Vogus. 2012. "Venturing for Others with Heart and Head: How Compassion Encourages Social Entrepreneurship." *Academy of Management Review* 37, no. 4, pp. 616–640.

Porter, M.E., and M. Kramer. 2011. "Creating Shared Value: How to Fix Capitalism and Unleash a New Wave of Growth." *Harvard Business Review* 89, pp. 62–77.

Rindova, V., D. Barry, and D. Ketchen. 2009. "Entrepreneuring as Emancipation." *Academy of Management Review* 34, no. 3, pp. 477–491.

Scott, R. 1995. *Institutions and Organizations.* Thousand Oaks, CA: Sage.

Shane, S., and S. Venkataraman. 2000. "The Promise of Entrepreneurship as a Field of Research." *Academy of Management Review* 25, no. 1, pp. 217–226.

Shaw, E., and S. Carter. 2007. "Social Entrepreneurship." *Journal of Small Business and Enterprise Development* 14, no. 3, pp. 418–434.

Stake, R. 1994. "Case Studies." In *Handbook of Qualitative Research,* eds. N. Denzin and Y. Lincoln. Thousand Oaks, CA: Sage.

Sternberg, R. 1988. *The Triarchic Mind: A New Theory of Human Intelligence.* New York: Viking.

Sternberg, R. 1997. *Successful Intelligence.* New York: Plume.

Sternberg, R. 2000. "Cross-Disciplinary Verification of Theories: The Case of the Triarchic Theory." *History of Psychology* 3, no. 3, pp. 177–179.

Sternberg, R. 2004. "Successful Intelligence as a Basis for Entrepreneurship." *Journal of Business Venturing* 19, no. 2, pp. 189–201.

Sternberg, R., G. Forsythe, J. Hedlund, R. Wagner, W. Williams, S. Snook, and E. Grigorienko. 2000. *Practical Intelligence in Everyday Life.* New York: Cambridge University Press.

Steyaert, C. 2007. "'Entrepreneuring' as a Conceptual Attractor? A Review of Process Theories in 20 Years of Entrepreneurship Studies." *Entrepreneurship and Regional Development* 19, no. 6, pp. 453–477.

Taylor, S., and R. Bogdan. 1984. *Introduction to Qualitative Research Methods: The Search for Meanings.* New York: Wiley.

Weber, M. 1968. *Economy and Society.* New York: Bedminster.

CHAPTER 2

I Think Therefore I Am ... Social Entrepreneurial Identity and Network Development

William Wales

University at Albany, State University of New York

Christopher Stein

University of Central Florida

Overview and Background

This experiential exercise was developed as a means to get students to understand and actively construct their social entrepreneurial identities through reflection and networking. The exercise enhances the social entrepreneurship content of an individual's professional network and generates deep-seated, yet practical, insight into the value of professional networking for social entrepreneurial identity development. It also enhances individuals' "role identity" as social entrepreneurs through incorporating reflections on personal social entrepreneurial objectives within their professional public images, identifying social entrepreneurial heroes, and choosing to participate in one or more social movement groups.

Learning Objectives

To develop positive self-image, social identity, self-confidence, interpersonal skills, and robust, supportive network that social entrepreneurs need to be successful.

Purpose/Learning Objectives

Networking has long been recognized as an important element of the entrepreneurial process in general (Aldrich and Zimmer 1986; Dacin, Dacin, and Tracey 2011) and of social entrepreneurship in particular (Prokesch, 2011). In a powerful recanting of the story of Kathy Giusti, founder of the Multiple Myeloma Research foundation, it is noted that after her diagnosis with multiple myeloma, she was unsure of how to act upon her desire to fight the disease and help make a lasting social impact. In the words of the author:

> She quickly realized that she had a powerful personal network that she could tap, including her sister, then a lawyer at Time Inc.; Heller, her boss and mentor at Searle; and her Harvard Business School classmates. An HBS alumni group helped her create her first business plan. (Prokesch, 2011)

In the case of Kathy Giusti, like many social entrepreneurs, her network made all the difference with her decision to become a social entrepreneur. Networks provide individuals with social support and resource access that enable their entrepreneurial ambitions to reach reality (Aldrich and Zimmer, 1986). However, perhaps even more significantly, they may also meaningfully influence an individual's "role identity," or how individuals "see themselves as entrepreneurs" (Krueger, 2007). Role identity, such as internalizing the notion that "I am a social entrepreneur," is a social construction based upon action, insight, and reflection. In this learning exercise, individuals are challenged to build the content of their professional image, objectives, and social network to better reflect their social entrepreneurial ambitions. In doing so, this exercise will help meaningfully enhance one's identity as a social entrepreneur. By shaping the narrative of one's professional image to put forth a more socially conscious image when engaging in professional networking, individuals may enhance their social entrepreneurial self-concept, activity level, and personal commitment, which meaningfully impact how they see themselves as social entrepreneurs (Krueger, 2007). Moreover, one's identity as a social entrepreneur may also be enhanced through joining and interacting with social movement organizations and admirable activists. By interacting with these communities and thought leaders, individuals have the opportunity to identify with peers as well as potential social entrepreneurial mentors, which further shape one's identity as a social entrepreneur (Dacin, Dacin, and Tracey 2011).

Time Required

Conducting this exercise may take up to an entire class section; however shorter versions of this exercise with less discussion are certainly possible. While not required, computers (or smartphones/tablets) and a reliable Internet connection are necessary if professional networking is to be conducted online during class. If these materials are not available, the exercise may be spread out over two class sessions with the in-person networking tasks assigned as homework between the two sessions (check with your instructor).

Exercise Schedule

The exercise has five major components: (1) Initial reflection on past social entrepreneurial activities and future objectives; (2) Crafting a professional objective statement that harmoniously emphasizes social and economic objectives; (3) Identifying and connecting with one or more high-potential "weak ties" [4] in your social entrepreneurial ecosystem; (4) Identifying and reaching out to a potential social entrepreneurial "hero" with a brief note, and joining one or more social movement organizations; and finally, (5) Debrief and closing reflection/discussion about the importance of developing one's social entrepreneurial identity.

Assignment

There are six steps to this exercise.

1. Prework

   For this exercise, you will be expected to develop your social entrepreneurial identity through professional networking and thoughtful development of your professional image. The emerging belief is that social identity and image are highly important considerations for social entrepreneurs (Dacin, Dacin, and Tracey 2011). As Dacin and colleagues articulate, when others recognize and explicitly acknowledge that an individual possesses a certain identity, that person's behavior is meaningfully shaped in a manner that better exemplifies the expectations of that identity (Dacin, Dacin, and Tracey 2011). When one changes their professional image and begins to use that image in public profiles such as resumes and online networking sites, they are more likely to promote and conform to a social identity that stimulates productive social entrepreneurial behavior. Moreover, once someone develops a strong social identity, their increased perceived legitimacy (in relation to stereotypes, etc.) enables greater opportunities and resource access for them when seeking support for their efforts. Therefore, while networking may have other broader benefits for facilitating social entrepreneurship (Aldrich and Zimmer, 1986), a deeper consideration pertains to social entrepreneurial identity development and its important consequences for social entrepreneurial behavior.

2. Opening reflection on your social entrepreneurial ideals

   The exercise begins with individual reflection on one's past social entrepreneurial deeds and future objectives. In a broad sense, the goal is to think about times when you have worked to help solve a social problem and/or bring about social change. It is likely that you may have not come up with an innovation in the way a particular social problem is being solved, but rather worked as part of an organization that has an established means of achieving social impact. Please conduct a "two-minute" essay in which you write (or type) for two minutes straight while answering the question, "Describe an instance or instances in which you devoted time to help solve a problem society faces, or bring about social change." It is OK to think outside the box in terms of what constitutes a problem that society faces. Keep in mind that a key aspect of the social entrepreneur's job is to identify a social problem in need of attention.

Once you have completed this, please begin a second "two-minute" essay where you write what comes to mind about what your future goals might be as a social entrepreneur. These goals need not be obtainable in the immediate future, but may be lofty ambitions that may take many years to accomplish. *Please give consideration to how these social goals might harmonize with your economic life goals.* What balance between social and economic impact do you see in your life? Please keep in mind that these essays are individual reflective activities that should be done in silence for the next few minutes. Following completion of the "essays," you will be asked to pair with one or more peer individuals to state your goals publicly and gain feedback from peers.

3. Crafting your personal social narrative

Next you are asked to reflect upon your peer feedback and to craft a more carefully worded personal social narrative about your professional objectives. You will be asked to place this narrative on your resume and/or professional online networking profile, that is, a LinkedIn profile—a premier online professional networking platform. In any case, you are now tasked with refining a carefully worded personal summary, or objective statement, which harmoniously emphasizes your social and economic goals. Crafting this statement generally causes one to think deeply about their social and economic career objectives. Please keep in mind that having a social impact is not incompatible with generating personal gains, and note that much of traditional entrepreneurial activity can be conceived as advancing social goals (Choi and Majumdar 2014). At this point, it is important to also emphasize that research in positive psychology on individual well-being suggests that satisfaction with life is tied to, among other factors, how meaningful we feel our work is, and that we all must define what personally constitutes a meaningful life (Seligman, 2011).

4. Discussions with "weak ties" in your social entrepreneurial network

The next segment of the activity involves challenging yourself to identify, connect with, and request to meet one or more high-potential weak ties in your social entrepreneurial network. Weak ties are individuals that you presently don't know very well but who might be influential experts, gatekeepers, or resource providers that may help "open doors" for you or enlighten your future social entrepreneurial endeavors (Granovetter 1973). These individuals may be new friends, friends-of-friends, parents-of-friends, former guest speakers, previous managers, teachers, neighbors, or other contacts that you've met in passing. There is also no harm in "blind" networking, or sending a "cold call or connection request" to even the most senior of individuals in the social entrepreneurial ecosystem. If online tools that facilitate instant contact requests are not available, you may work on developing a strategy to meet with, and perhaps interview, one of your high-potential weak ties over the next few days. Your goal at this stage is simply to leverage your personally constructed social narrative and goals in a more public setting. Weak ties working in the social entrepreneurial ecosystem are likely to provide important insights, encouragement, and mentoring, which may help you further craft your personal narrative and objectives.

5. Identify social entrepreneurial heroes and organizations

The next segment of the exercise challenges you to consider whom you consider to be your entrepreneurial hero (or heroes). Who do you admire? Might this individual be someone in your network of "weak ties"? If so, might they be willing to be your mentor? Most people are inclined to respond favorably if you ask them for their help when you promise to be respectful of their time. It is important to recognize that it is OK to have social entrepreneurial "heroes" and they help shape one's understanding and identity as a social entrepreneur (Dacin, Dacin, and Tracey 2011). Please develop a strategy for *contacting* your social entrepreneurial hero. If this strategy involves technological tools such as e-mail, Twitter, Linked In, or telephone, and these tools are available, please take the time now to reach out via one of these electronic mediums to your identified hero. While you may not receive a response, it is nonetheless thoughtful and gratifying to convey your admiration.

Second, at this stage of the exercise, please give consideration to a social movement organization that you are willing to commit to becoming a part of for at least their next few in-person meetings or online webinars. Embedding yourself within a social movement group is highly influential to gaining the support and insight one needs to "not feel like you're on your own" and to persevere as a social entrepreneur when the journey seems to have more ups than downs. While "live" or in-person groups may better satisfy the goals of this activity, if online networks are being used for this exercise, many social movement organizations (that is, LinkedIn groups, such as the Schwab Foundation for Social Entrepreneurship) may be searched and joined rather quickly. However, please note that while more than 450 social entrepreneurship groups are joinable, many are private and you must request permission to join. Please note that online groups should however be seen as supplementary and secondary to joining in-person groups.

6. Closing reflection on your social entrepreneurial identity

The final stage of this exercise consists of a debriefing, reflection, and discussion about your social entrepreneurial identity and future social entrepreneurial goals. Please begin with a "one-minute" essay in which you type (or write) for one minute straight reflecting on the following questions: (1) What have you learned about your social entrepreneurial identity personally? (2) How will your networking efforts continue to shape your identity? Please be prepared to read your personal objective statements to the class. Please be prepared to discuss the individuals and types of people that you identified as high-potential weak ties along with what social movement organizations or notable social entrepreneurial individuals you sought to contact or join.

References and Additional Resources

Aldrich, H.E., and C. Zimmer. 1986. "Entrepreneurship Through Social Networks." In *The Art and Science of Entrepreneurship,* eds. D. Sexton and R. Smilor, 3–23. New York: Ballinger.

Choi, N., and S. Majumdar. 2014. "Social Entrepreneurship as an Essentially Contested Concept: Opening a New Avenue for Systematic Future Research." *Journal of Business Venturing* 29, no. 3, pp. 363–76.

Dacin, M.T., P.A. Dacin, and P. Tracey. 2011. "Social Entrepreneurship: A Critique and Future Directions." *Organization Science* 22, no. 5, pp. 1203–13.

Granovetter, M.S. 1973. "The Strength of Weak Ties." *The American Journal of Sociology* 78, no. 6, pp. 1360–80.

Krueger, N.F. 2007. "What Lies Beneath? The Experiential Essence of Entrepreneurial Thinking." *Entrepreneurship Theory and Practice* 31, no. 1, pp. 123–38.

Prokesch, S. 2011. "The Reluctant Social Entrepreneur." *Harvard Business Review* 89, no. 6, pp. 124–126.

Seligman, M. 2011. *Flourish: A Visionary New Understanding of Happiness and Well-being.* New York: Atria Books.

CHAPTER 3

Purpose versus Profits

Jerrid P. Kalakay

Valencia College

Introduction

This exercise helps students develop a deeper understanding of the various missions associated with social entrepreneurship. It furthers the development of students' social entrepreneurial skill-set and their understanding of decision making regarding social value and wealth creation.

Purpose/Learning Objectives

Decision making within business dating back to the 1950s with Herbert Simon's (1959) studies often overlaps between economics and psychology. Organizational decision making has been investigated from the frames of ethics, rationality, moral philosophy, culture, and cognitive moral development among many others (Jones 1991; Loe et al. 2000; Simon 1959, 1979). Through these various frames, organizational decision making has continued to be of interest to many scholars and practitioners. Decision making within social entrepreneurship can be even more complex with the introduction of the multiple organizational missions of social value and wealth creation. These dual missions within social enterprises force social entrepreneurs with the additional mission-driven criteria of purpose and profit to their decisions. Purpose is defined as creating social value for the public good, and profit is defined as creating profitable operations resulting in private gain (Austin, et al. 2006). This exercise allows students to make the distinction between a purpose-driven decision and a profit-driven decision through five unique fictional cases that a social entrepreneur has made while navigating the enterprise. Obviously, in practice, these decisions are rarely as binary as this exercise would suggest; however, it is intended to spawn conversation and further student understanding on the complexity of decision making within social enterprises.

Time Required

Conducting this exercise will likely take two hours from an entire class session. While not required, a computer with a projector is necessary if the cases are presented instead of provided only as a hard copy (check with your instructor).

Exercise Schedule

The exercise has five major components: (1) Individual reading of each case; (2) Individual sorting of cases by purpose-driven decisions and profit driven decisions complete with reasoning; (3) Share in pairs your reasoning for your sorting and try to reach consensus with your partner on sortings; (4) Participate in a class discussion on each case and its respective sorting; and (5) Conduct a debriefing and reflection session on the cases and the subsequent discussions.

Assignment

1. Pre-reading and preparation work
   For this exercise, you will be expected to read the assigned articles and brainstorm some purpose-driven decisions and profit-driven decisions, respectively.

   • Ashoka, "Scouting the Sweet Spot Between Purpose and Profit" www.forbes.com/sites/ashoka/2013/02/12/scouting-the-sweet-spot-between-purpose-and-profit/#556a4e9f3953.
   • Birkinshaw, J., N.J. Foss, and S. Lindenberg. "Combining Purpose with Profits," http://sloanreview.mit.edu/article/combining-purpose-with-profits/.

2. Sorting of decisions
   Sort the decision in each case by the categories of purpose-driven versus profit-driven. You will have between 10 and 15 minutes in

total to complete your sorting of the decisions into their respective categories. It is desired to have all 5 in one category or the other and not to sort any as in between. Although in the real world, there is likely quite a bit of "gray" area regarding these decisions, this exercise is intended to generate discussion on each case from binary sorting.

3. Group share

In pairs of two, share your respective sorting (groups can be larger than two at the discretion of your instructor). After you and your partner(s) have shared your reasoning for sorting each case decision into its respective category, try and reach a consensus between lists. This process should be focused on understanding your partner's/ partners' reasoning while also articulating your own reasoning on any differences.

4. Class discussion

The class discussion further expands the conversations you were having in your group to include even more points of view of your classmates and instructor. This process, similarly as in the group discussion, should be focused on understanding different perspectives while articulating your own.

5. Debriefing and reflection

The true value of this exercise comes from the knowledge and experience gained from articulating your perspective on the cases while also gaining insights into other perspectives. This is only realized upon a careful debrief and reflection session with the class. This debrief should be taken seriously and facilitated by your Instructor.

References and Additional Resources

Austin, J., H. Stevenson, and J. Wei-Skillern. 2006. "Social and Commercial Entrepreneurship: Same, Different, or Both?" *Entrepreneurship Theory and Practice* 30, no. 1, pp. 1–22.

Jones, T. 1991. "Ethical Decision Making by Individuals in Organizations: An Issue-Contingent Model." *Academy of Management Review* 16, no. 2, pp. 366–395.

Loe, T., L. Ferrell, and P. Mansfield. 2000. "A Review of Empirical Studies Assessing Ethical Decision Making in Business." *Journal of Business Ethics* 25, no. 3, pp. 185–204.

Simon, H. 1959. "Theories of Decision-Making in Economics and Behavioral Science." *The American Economic Review* 49, no. 3, pp. 253–283.

Simon, H. 1979. "Rational Decision Making in Business Organizations." *The American Economic Review* 69, no. 4, pp. 493–513.

CHAPTER 4

Free Geek Toronto: Tradeoffs in Open Source and Triple Bottom Line Organizations

Ushnish Sengupta

University of Toronto

Introduction

There is a trend in social enterprise in developing intellectual property through practice, and subsequently monetizing the intellectual property to generate revenue. A case study of Free Geek provides a counterexample to this trend, describing an open source, triple bottom line organization that scales its impact by licensing its intellectual property at no financial cost. In particular, this chapter describes the startup process of Free Geek Toronto (*FGT*), which is modeled on Free Geek Portland and Free Geek Vancouver, which are "open source" organizations, which indicates that the organizational structure and content is published freely for any organization in the world to replicate through a social franchise model. FGT is a formally incorporated nonprofit organization and a social enterprise, and its mission includes: increasing access to computing and communications technologies; providing education, training, and job skills; promoting the use of Free and Open Source Software (FOSS); and reducing the environmental impact of electronic waste.

This chapter outlines the opportunities and challenges faced by FGT, a social enterprise located in the junction neighborhood of Toronto. FGT is modeled on a successful organization called Free Geek in Portland, Oregon, which is a triple bottom line organization, embodying social, environmental, and financial goals (http://www.freegeek.org/). The social bottom line involves reducing the digital divide by providing no-cost and low-cost computers to individuals who cannot afford new computers. The environmental bottom line is the reduction of e-waste sent to landfills, by reusing usable computer components and recycling other components. The financial bottom line involves ensuring the organization is financial sustainable through earned revenues.

Open Source Organizations

Free Geek is an "open source" organization that allows any other organization to adopt its organizational "blueprint," apply it to another organization, modify it, and improve it. The open source principle is based on the FOSS movement, which enables individuals to copy, modify, and redistribute software applications through "CopyLeft" licenses such as Creative Commons (which as the name suggests is fundamentally different from copyright). Free Geek also enables other organizations to learn from both successes and failures, by posting organizational documents including the minutes of every meeting on a publicly accessible website. Free Greek publishes a detailed organizational model on the Internet, freely available for anyone to use under the Creative Commons license. The trademarked name "Free Geek" can be used if organizations agree to follow a number of nonmonetary requirements, such as the free and open source software and democratic decision making advice. This Open Source, Social Franchise business model enables Free Geek to replicate the model in different locations with low administrative overhead. Since Free Geek started in Portland 10 years ago, nine other Free Geeks have started up in different cities, including Free Geek Vancouver. FGT applied and was accepted by Free Geek as the "official" Free Geek Toronto. FGT's mission and vision are closely aligned with the overall Free Geek model, although the geographical, and national, regional and local government context is different.

Free Geek Toronto

1. Mission, vision, and activities

FGT's Mission is: "To promote social and economic justice by: increasing access to computing and communications technologies; providing access to education, training and job skills, promoting the use of Free and Open Source Software, and reducing the environmental impact of electronic waste." Its Vision for the future is to make our city a place where e-waste is disposed of responsibly, safely, and ethically, and where everyone has access to computers and Internet. FGT has established a community technology center in the junction neighborhood of Toronto. This center operates the following primary activities:

- Trains volunteers to safely dismantle older computers, recover reusable parts, and to rebuild them as a computer technician would do
- Empowers these volunteers in the installation, use, and benefits of Ubuntu, a free and open source Linux distribution known for its ease of use,
- Provides public access to computers and the Internet
- Serves as a recycling depot for people who need to get rid of old computers
- Provides graduates of this program with opportunities to receive further training and part-time paid employment to refurbish computers
- Incorporates an in-house Thrift Store where excess refurbished systems, peripherals, and components will be sold and
- Ensures that leftover e-waste will be sold only to local, ethical downstream recycling plants.

2. The Junction community

The geographical area where the majority of FGT's members reside is Toronto's "Junction" neighborhood. Although the Junction is not Toronto's poorest neighborhood, it is a neighborhood with a high proportion of low-income households (United Way of Greater Toronto and the Canadian Council on Social Development, 2004). There are a significant number of individuals whose primary income is from government social support programs including Ontario Welfare (OW) or Ontario Disability Support Program (ODSP), who reside in the Junction neighborhood due to affordable rental housing and the availability of services such as public transit.

A neighborhood with an increasing number of individuals who have lost employment from the steady decline in blue-collar jobs combined with people who are on OW or ODSP provides a strong impetus for starting new community development organizations. The Junction neighborhood provides social entrepreneurs and community organizers with a "stable but inherently unjust equilibrium" (Martin and Osberg 2007), which requires new organizations and projects to correct or mitigate the imbalance. One such imbalance is the high proportion of income-poor individuals who do not have a computer at home. The lack of a home computer and Internet access limits the possibilities for engagement in employment search, self-employment, civic participation, and community activities.

3. History of the organization

A number of social entrepreneurs who recognized an unjust equilibrium in access to computers for income-poor individuals in Toronto identified the Free Geek Portland's organizational model as one that can be replicated in Toronto. The group of individuals who were interested in developing a Free Geek in Toronto had another common interest: involvement in Toronto's Free Open Source software community. Through a number of attempts to start up the organization with different groups of people, the right mix of cofounders was developed by 2009. The social entrepreneurs who started FGT had sufficient social capital to start a new organization and took a community rather than individualistic approach to starting up the organization. The social capital available to the social entrepreneurs consisted of strong social networks including family and friends, and weak social networks consisting of connections from previous employment and volunteer projects (Granovetter 1973).

4. Target population

   As a social enterprise (Quarter and Armstrong 2009), FGT focuses on the lowest quartile of income groups as defined by Statistics Canada, with the very lowest subgroup of that quartile that are on social assistance, either in the form of OW or the ODSP. FGT's target population is the income-poor. FGT gives them the hardware, software, and desktop training they need to participate more fully in society, and thus raise their computer literacy and the self-esteem. FGT does not charge any financial cost for one new computer a year for volunteers, allowing income-poor individuals to reserve most of their income for food, rent, and other essentials. The income-poor and hard-to-employ are often shuffled from one training or volunteer program to the next, never getting the opportunity to apply what they have learned in a workplace setting, and thereby largely forgetting the training acquired. FGT provides hands-on and carry-on environments for people to develop, retain, and grow their technical, organizational, and communication skills.

5. The enabling possibilities of FOSS

   FGT installs FOSS on the computers that are grants to volunteers and also on the computers it sells through the Thrift store. There are a number of advantages to using Open Source software, including lowering financial barriers though installation of free software, and lowering participation barriers by enabling users to become valuable contributors in the OSS community, and a growing niche market.

   The total lifecycle cost of using proprietary software is not only the initial installation whether at a low subsidized cost, donated, or pirated; there is a lifetime of costs for upgrades and potential support. This lifetime cost can be a significant factor for those on low income in being further disenfranchised through a digital divide. FOSS lowers the financial barrier to participation in an increasingly digital economy and society.

   Any contribution to improving proprietary software is necessarily limited, and the primarily financial benefits are to an organization, not to any individual. Individual contributions to OSS are recognized, and may even enable people to get employment and self-employment over the long term. Mel Chua described her journey of transformation from a user to a contributor in a presentation titled "The Invisible Traceback: Blockers that make potential contributors drop out (and how to fix them)" (Chua 2009).

The final advantage is the ability for FGT to develop and maintain a niche market of expertise in Linux operating systems, as the services in the dominant and Windows market are overcrowded. Free Geek offers Linux-based courses, Linux-based computer installations for offices and schools, and plans to provide Linux-based consulting services.

6. An evolving governance structure

FGT was incorporated as a nonprofit corporation without share capital, and plans to work though the multi-year process to become a registered charity in Canada. FGT is a democratically run, membership-driven, and worker-driven organization. The members contribute time and work, instead of financial dues. Within the membership, there are some distinctions:

- *Board of Directors:* Chosen by members; provide legal and financial oversight.
- *Council:* Policy and important decisions are made at monthly general meetings of the members, through a consensus decision-making process.
- *Staff Collective:* Full-time and part-time employees paid by FGT.
- *Core, Adoption, & Build Volunteers:* Different levels based on time commitments.

The transition from an informal "club" of volunteers to an incorporated organization with a board of directors was difficult for FGT. Prior to incorporation, the council was the de facto "board" for the organization, making important policy decisions. The council has practiced and recently adopted formal consensus (Butler and Rothstein 2007). Formal consensus has the promise of being a more democratic process than supervisor–employee or Roberts Rules of Order processes. Formal consensus attempts to improve a proposal through addressing questions and concerns rather than adversarial votes for and against a motion as in Robert's Rules of Order.

7. Volunteer involvement in business operations

Both paid and volunteer participants perform most of the day-to-day work, including dismantling, testing, building, sales, training, and support. They also work within workgroups and the Council for group decision making. Future staff will be chosen from amongst the core group of volunteers. Staff and volunteers are encouraged to both peer-teach and pursue the development of new skills.

One of the differences between FGT and more hierarchical organizations is the greater role of volunteers. In a typical hierarchical nonprofit organization, there is an Executive Director managing staff, who in turn manages volunteers. FGT started off as a volunteer-member managed organization and had no Executive Director. The president of the board performed Executive Director functions, and a separate Executive Director position was later created and filled. Volunteer members are involved in hiring staff through workgroups and provide overall guidance to staff through council meetings.

Another difference between FGT and other volunteer-involving organizations is that a significant number of the volunteers at FGT are also recipients of products/services. Volunteers involved in the adopting and building programs are granted a computer to take home upon completing the required hours of service. Volunteers who have received a computer through a grant or have purchased a computer (at an extremely low cost of $50) also receive technical support services. All members and volunteers can attend a wide variety of training courses completely free of charge.

8. Tradeoffs between social, environmental, and financial goals

FGT faces tradeoffs between its social mission and economic self-sufficiency objectives. The organization takes in donations of used computer equipment, refurbishes the equipment, and grants the equipment at no cost to individuals who cannot afford new computers. FGT also sells used computers to support its operations. Therefore, there is a tradeoff between the social goals supported by granting computers and the economic goals supported by selling the same computers. One solution implemented to moderate the demand for granted computers is the substantial hours of volunteering requirement to receive a free computer. Therefore, by implementing a "teach a person to fish" model rather than a "give a person a fish" model, FGT has been able to fulfill its primary social mission while also having the ability to sell computers to support economic objectives.

As a triple bottom line enterprise, FGT also faces tradeoffs between environmental goals and economic goals. The organization follows a "reduce, reuse and recycle" philosophy by reusing every possible working computer component and recycling the remainder. Recyclable materials can be sold to processors, some of which are global traders who are able to provide a high price for recyclable materials. But the material recovery practices they use are questionable in terms of employee health and safety and environmental disposal practices, particularly with cheaper labor used in developing countries. Therefore, there is a tradeoff for getting a higher price for recyclable materials from questionable processors, or a lower price in working with more environmentally sustainable processors. The solution implemented by FGT is to join a provincial waste stewardship program, which certifies electronic waste processors in Ontario, and provides a reasonable price for collecting electronic waste.

Finally, there is a tradeoff between social and environmental goals. The largest expenses for the enterprise are rent and staff. Therefore, the utilization of space and staff resources can be divided between social objectives such as computer classes, and environmental objectives such as electronic waste recycling. FGT has struck a balance between these two objectives by creating a multifunctional space and specialized staff roles. Desks have been set up with power and Internet connections that can be used for holding educational classes as well as computer recycling activities.

9. Summary

FGT's opportunities and challenges described in this chapter include the adoption of the open source Free Geek organizational model, the enabling possibilities of open source software, and governance challenges in transition from a club of individuals to an incorporated entity with a board of directors. The process for overcoming governance challenges for FGT include recruiting new board members who will be part of a generative problem-solving board rather than a policy-making board (Chait, Ryan, and Taylor 2011). As a social enterprise, the long-term viability of the organization will depend on the delicate balance between social environmental and financial goals of the organization. Broadening the member base to include a greater number of volunteers, one of the most undervalued resources, will enable the organization to build its human and social capital to work through current and future challenges.

Case Study Questions

1. What are some different examples of organizations with Open Source business models in your region?
2. Does the concept of Open Source, which is successful for software applications, translate to different types of social enterprise?
3. How would you structure the social franchise of Free Geek so it can replicate itself and increase social and environmental impact across different contexts?
4. What are the contextual factors that enable or hinder replication of a social enterprise and how would you restructure FGT to match the local contextual factors, while replicating the Free Geek Model?
5. How would you manage the strategy and operations for FGT to balance achievement of all three elements of the triple bottom line?
6. What long-term strategies would you develop to achieve FGTs long-term goals for social enterprise: and what operational policies, procedures, and practices would you implement to achieve FGTs long-term goals?
7. How would you develop the appropriate culture for volunteers, staff, and board members to enable the highest level of participation by all organizational constituents keeping in mind your social mission?

References and Additional Resources

Butler, C.T.L., and A. Rothstein. 2007. *On Conflict and Consensus: A Handbook on Formal Consensus Decisionmaking*, 3rd ed. Mountain View, CA: Creative Commons.

Chait, R.P., W.P. Ryan, and B.E. Taylor. 2011. *Governance as Leadership: Reframing the Work of Nonprofit Boards*. Hoboken, NJ: John Wiley & Sons.

Chua, M. 2009. "The Invisible Traceback: Blockers that Make Potential Contributors Drop Out (and How to Fix Them)." presentation at the Ontario [GNU] Linuxfest www.linuxpromagazine.com/Online/Blogs/ROSE-Blog-Rikki-s-Open-Source-Exchange/ROSE-Blog-Interviews-Red-Hat-s-Mel-Chua (accessed April 15, 2015).

Free Geek Portland Website www.freegeek.org/ (accessed April 15, 2015).

Free Geek Toronto Website http://freegeektoronto.org/ (accessed April 15, 2015).

Granovetter, M.S. 1973. "The Strength of Weak Ties." *American Journal of Sociology* 78, no. 6, pp. 1360–80.

Martin, R.L., and S. Osberg. 2007. "Social Entrepreneurship: The Case for Definition." *Stanford Social Innovation Review* (Spring) 5, no. 2, pp. 29–39.

Quarter, J.M.L., and A. Armstrong. 2009. *Understanding the Social Economy: A Canadian Perspective*. Toronto: University of Toronto Press.

United Way of Greater Toronto and the Canadian Council on Social Development. 2004. *Poverty By Postal Code: The Geography of Neighbourhood Poverty*, pp. 1981–2001.

CHAPTER 5

Worksheet for "Defining Social Entrepreneurship"

Paul Miesing

University at Albany, State University of New York

Am I a Social Entrepreneur?

There is no magic formula to be a social entrepreneur and there are no quick steps to succeed. Read the following statements and rate each on the **1–4** scale. As you do so, please keep in mind that there are no "best answers." While individuals will feel differently about these statements, each of us instinctively tends to have a natural bias toward some of them. Moreover, these are your self-perceptions and might not reflect reality. They are only to give you an understanding of your strengths and areas to focus on in your entrepreneurial development; your responses do not predict whether you will succeed or fail.

	Strongly disagree	Slightly disagree	Slightly agree	Strongly agree
1. Business has a role to play in addressing societal issues.	1	2	3	4
2. Business performance should be measured in terms of its impact on society.	1	2	3	4
3. Given my sense of urgency and individual responsibility, I want large change now.	1	2	3	4

(Continued)

	Strongly disagree	Slightly disagree	Slightly agree	Strongly agree
4. I am concerned about consequences that are due to my actions or attitudes.	1	2	3	4
5. I am concerned about what happens in society.	1	2	3	4
6. I am keenly interested in managing for maximum value and impact as a leader.	1	2	3	4
7. I am passionate about social justice.	1	2	3	4
8. I am persistent in relentlessly pursuing my vision and rarely take no for an answer.	1	2	3	4
9. I have a strong conviction about my role in my community or in society.	1	2	3	4
10. I have goals for my venture beyond making money.	1	2	3	4
11. I know I can't do it all myself, so partnerships and alliances are important to succeed.	1	2	3	4
12. I measure performance by taking into account a positive return to society such as furthering broad social, cultural, and environmental goals.	1	2	3	4
13. I view social issues as an opportunity to transform society for the better.	1	2	3	4
14. I want to create systemic, sustainable impact that yields long-term benefits to everyone by starting my own business enterprise.	1	2	3	4
15. I want to invent new approaches and identify practical solutions to problems in our society.	1	2	3	4

(Continued)

	Strongly disagree	Slightly disagree	Slightly agree	Strongly agree
16. I want to pursue a suitable solution to social problems.	1	2	3	4
17. I want to understand the social, political, and cultural context of my business in addition to the economic.	1	2	3	4
18. It is important that I give back to my community.	1	2	3	4
19. My values—and not profits *per se*—influence what I want out of developing and running an enterprise.	1	2	3	4
20. Others consider me to be unreasonable but I think I'm passionate.	1	2	3	4
21. Social problems are often the result of market and institutional failures, but they can be corrected by business.	1	2	3	4
22. The line is blurring between profit and nonprofit, business and charity.	1	2	3	4
23. There is a huge business opportunity in helping the billions of people around the world who cannot afford to participate in the market.	1	2	3	4
24. Value lies in the social benefit to a community or transformation of a community that lacks the resources to fulfill its own needs.	1	2	3	4
25. Wealth should be merely a tool to effect social change and not an end in itself.	1	2	3	4
Totals:				
Overall Average =				

After you have completed this assessment, add up your score and calculate the average.

1–1.2	1.3–2.0	2.1–2.9	3.0–3.7	3.8–4
Your social entrepreneurial drive needs work. It may take some time for you to develop the abilities and attitudes that are necessary to succeed.	Most people fall in this range. Social entrepreneurship may create more stress for you than it is worth. You might be better off working for someone else.	You may have the ability to be a social entrepreneur, but consider additional training to develop your skills and deal with the inevitable problems and stress.	Your personal characteristics give you a satisfactory ability to be a successful social entrepreneur.	You have many characteristics that could make you a great social entrepreneur including the desire, energy, and adaptability to make a social venture succeed.

PART II

Contexts for Social Entrepreneurs

CHAPTER 6

Recognizing and Reframing Social Problems into Business Opportunities: MECE and Value Chain Analysis*

Sunny Jeong

Wittenberg University

Introduction

Problem is an opportunity for a social entrepreneur. You should be able to "connect the dots" among people's daily lived/living experiences and surrounding environments, any incomplete or mal-directed solutions offered by markets, government policies, nonprofits. Stories of a particular community in Rwanda (reading of today's session) provide you a rich context of people's daily lives and a typical NGO's solution that worsened problems. In this exercise, you will acknowledge the complexity of social problems in any given society, and at the same time (1) learn ways to untangle them into pieces where solutions are sought possible and (2) understand benefits of market-driven solutions. Toward the end of this exercise, you will be ready to learn comprehensive business models of social entrepreneurs.

First, you will review the previous lesson (the current module is prepared after learning the challenges of (global) social problems followed by

---

* This exercise uses an excerpt ("Empowering Women in Rwanda") from Jacqueline Novogratz, J. (2009). *The Blue Sweater: Bridging the Gap Between Rich and Poor in an Interconnected World* (New York: Rodale).

learning a business model), which explored that it is important to ask *why* before *how* to solve a problem. What really causes certain social problems is often more critical than hastily browsing solutions to problems that only appear superficially. Today, you will learn two analytical tools, McKinsey's Mutually Exclusive and Collectively Exhaustive framework (MECE) and Value Chain Analysis. You will apply them to a particular social problem in Rwanda (i.e., women's bread business project is failing). Again, understanding roots of the problem (primary focus on *why* question) will lead you to find solutions (*how* question) to those identified problems. MECE and Value Chain Analysis can be used as a guiding compass to identify opportunities to address social problems in any given society. You will work as a group, discuss, and write roots of problems, and solutions on a post-it easel pad prepared for each team. As working with your team, you will almost certainly get a richer answer than if you work on your own. Once your team identifies mutually exclusive and collectively exhaustive issues and ways to create and increase values in the Rwanda's community project case, you can then come up with ways to maximize this value whether through excellent human resources, superb products, great services, or jobs well done.

Purpose/Learning Objectives

- Understanding problems are opportunity identification for social entrepreneurs. You will learn how to analyze social problems by using business tools.
- Learn the MECE framework and Value Chain Analysis to identify social problems.
- Practice, exercise, and apply MECE and Value Chain Analysis to a specific NGO project prepared for this class so that you can fully grasp how to use them on other social problems.
- Learn the process of identifying (global) social problems, evaluating strategies to address those problems, and finally develop their capacity to translate innovative ideas for social change into marketplace solutions.
- Students focus on behavioral statements or activities to describe problems presented in a case so that problems can be perceived as and linked to actionable opportunities after all.

Group Size

- Any number of groups of preferably three to four members in each group.
- Instructor should walk around and participate in a group conversation to facilitate and guide if necessary.
- Each group will be assigned a white post-it easel paper and a marker. One person can facilitate a conversation by writing down their findings, solutions, results of discussions on the paper. All groups post their findings on the front board and a minimum of two teams (depending on minutes allowed) will present their findings.

Time Required

This exercise can be done comfortably with 2 class sessions of 60 minutes or within 80 minutes of one class session with a shorter version and a reading homework.

- Two class sessions of 60 minutes (plus prework and longer discussion or debriefing if desired) if lectures are given in class sessions and case is read during the second class session, followed by a group discussion.
- A minimum of 80 minutes if introduction and background of this exercise is announced in the previous class and reading is assigned as homework.
- Individual assignment: 20 minutes.

Reading (attached) of *The Blue Sweater* is handed out before the session, and students read a case before the class (or students can read individually in class if you have 2 sessions of 60 minutes).

- Group discussion and short presentation: 30 minutes.

Several groups volunteer to share their lists (15 minutes) and instructors comment on identified problems that are relevant to the business value chain.

- Wrap up, introduction of next session, business model:
10 minutes.

Exercise Schedule (2 Class Sessions of 60 Minutes Each)

The MECE framework and Value Chain Analysis are very useful analytical tools for students to understand that any tough social problem can be solved as long as we can dissect them into a subset of actionable issues to increase its value. The MECE principle is one of core consulting frameworks used by the McKinsey & Company consulting firm (*The McKinsey Way* by E.M. Rasiel) to solve a business problem. Value Chain Analysis involves a three-step process that helps you focus on activities (i.e., women did not change oils) instead of abstract problem (i.e., women provided poor products to their customers). There are three steps to this exercise.

1. Activity analysis

   The first step is to brainstorm the activities that Rwandan women undertook that in some way contribute toward poor customer experience and failure of their business. At an organizational level, this will include the step-by-step business process that you use to develop, produce your product, and serve your customer. These include production process of your product, input and output, marketing of your products, sales and order-taking, operational processes, delivery, customer service, accounting, human resource management, and so on. Once you have brainstormed activities which caused the poor performance of "bread business," list them on a paper. A useful way of listing them is to lay them out as a simplified flowchart running down the page—this gives a good visual representation of your "value chain." However, all listed activities should be mutually exclusive and collectively exhaustive.

2. Step 2: Value analysis

   Now, for each activity your team has identified, list the "value factors" that your customers appreciate in the way that each activity can be addressed. For example, if your team is talking about production of bread, your customer will value a fresh/healthy/delicious product. If your team is thinking about delivery of a product, your customer will most likely value an accurate and fast delivery, polite manner of the delivery person, and efficiency of eating bread over other lunch or snack options elsewhere.

Next to each activity you have identified, write down these value factors. And next to these, write down what needs to be improved and changed to provide greater value for each value factor.

3. Step 3: Evaluation and planning

Now, it is time to move on to action. Your team has analyzed ways to increase value in your business process. Pick out the quick, easy, and cheap solutions, and then evaluate others if they are practical. Also, it would be great to evaluate Jacqueline's solutions compared to yours. In which value chain process did she increase value for Rwanda's women business? Some solutions from your team will deliver great improvements, but at a great cost. If this is the case, drop them. Always take costs into consideration of any delivery of your value in a chain. Prioritize the remaining tasks and plan to tackle them in an achievable way that delivers higher value to customers, communities, and society they operate their business.

Empowering Women in Rwanda: The Blue Sweater by Jacqueline Novogratz[1]

An entrepreneur who is now the CEO of Acumen Fund, a nonprofit social venture capital fund that invests in businesses that bring solutions to low income people in the world, recently published a book called The Blue Sweater. Following is an excerpt from the book about working with a rural women's cooperative in Rwanda.

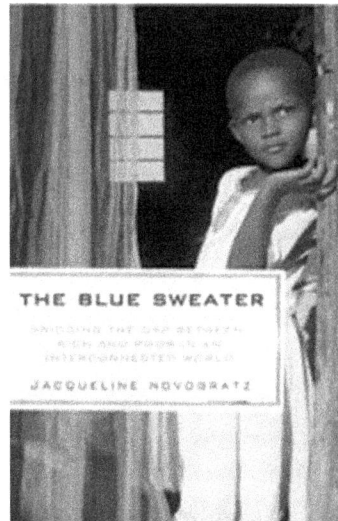

THE BLUE SWEATER

BRIDGING THE GAP BETWEEN RICH AND POOR IN AN INTERCONNECTED WORLD

JACQUELINE NOVOGRATZ

---

[1] Jacqueline Novogratz (2009). *The Blue Sweater: Bridging the Gap Between Rich and Poor in an Interconnected World* (New York: Rodale).

I wanted to see what it would take to make a business work in Rwanda. Honorata [a social worker] told me about a project she'd helped create for single mothers in Nyamirambo, the section of Kigali where lower-income people lived. "I've worked with them for years," Honorata told me. "The women have such good intentions, and you will like them."

The group, known as the "Femmes Seules"—or single women, code for unwed mothers—was one of many organized in part by Honorata's Ministry for Family and Social Affairs. The women, among the city's poorest, would gather for training and income generation. This group focused on a baking project and sewing dresses. In a moment, it was clear to me that "income generation" was not an accurate term. Only one woman was sewing; the rest were sitting and waiting.

There were about 20 of them, identically dressed in green smocks. Their dresses could have passed for prison attire.

I asked Prisca to help me understand the baked-goods project. "It's simple," she said. "Each morning, several women come very early to prepare the day's selection. It is always the same." I would come to know that selection better than I wanted to: *beignets* (fried lumps of dough), *batonnets* (the same dough molded into sticks and fried), *samosas*, tiny waffles, and hot tea. The women would take the goods to the govern-ment offices in the middle of the morning and sell them for 10 francs each. They'd then come back with whatever cash they'd earned and give it to Prisca.

In concept, I liked the idea. I knew from experience at UNICEF[2] that people would get hungry by 10:30 or 11:00 in the morning because everyone arrived at work at 7:30 and didn't have a break until lunch. There were no little stores selling snack foods, and people rarely brought treats from home. "How can I be of help?" I asked. Prisca answered, "The women are too poor. They earn too little money. They work every day, but the project is losing money."

"How much do the women earn?" I asked. "Fifty francs a day," Pri-sca responded—50 cents. "How much do you lose?" Prisca took out the ledger in which she recorded every franc spent, earned, and paid to the women. On average, the project was losing about $650 a month. "Who covers the losses?" I asked. "Two charities," Prisca said. "But I don't know how long they will renew our funding."

Six hundred and fifty dollars a month to keep 20 women earning 50 cents a day. You could triple their incomes if you gave them the money. It was a perfect illustration of why traditional charity too often fails: well-intentioned people gave poor women something "nice" to do and subsidized the project until there was no money left. This is a no-fail way to keep people in poverty. How would this survive in the long term? How would *the women* change their circumstances?

"Prisca, that's not enough," I said. "No," she said, visibly embarrassed, "it isn't." I was foolish to start with criticism. This is where so many Westerners fail: after a quick appraisal, we're ready to tell people in low-income communities not only what's wrong with what they're doing but also how to fix it. I apologized and tried again: "Could you be selling more? Could you cut costs?" They already had, Prisca explained; "it is easier to find more people to buy than to cut costs." "I'll make a deal with you," I said. "If we drop the charity and run this as a business, I'll help make it work." Our goals would be those of any business: to increase sales and cut costs. We'd start tomorrow and turn this project into a real enterprise.

I started early next morning. Without a common language, we communicated through gestures and sprinkled words of French or Swahili. While the women prepared for the morning, I reviewed the books more thoroughly than I had the previous afternoon. The bakery had a long way to go, but the feeling of starting something that had a chance of changing people's lives invigorated me. The world had written off this little group, yet they had a chance to do something important for themselves, and maybe they would change perceptions of what the poorest women are capable of accomplishing.

Because we started with 20 women, it made sense to expand our revenues quickly to cover costs. Rather than convince our few current customers to buy more doughnuts, we needed to increase the number of people we served. The only way I could think of achieving this was to target agencies and institutions with enough employees to make it worth our while to visit.

I asked Prisca to translate: "who will volunteer to come with me and speak with ambassadors and agency directors to see if they will offer our bakery services to their employees?" Twenty faces turned downward. "Don't worry," I said. "I'll do the talking, but you need to learn to market."

No movement. Consolata made the mistake of glancing up. I chose her. "What do you normally say to people in the offices when you want to sell to them?" I asked her. "Normally, I don't say anything," she nearly whispered. "I just walk through the government agencies and everyone knows what I'm carrying."

We visited five embassies and most UN agencies that first long day. We arrived at Nyamirambo exhausted, both of us content; we had doubled the number of customers. The next morning, I found the women hard at work, cooking doughnuts in a traditional wok-like pot over an open fire. I watched Josepha and the others choose their selections. They would walk into the street and disappear into a crowded minibus. For at least some, the new day took courage, for they were going to embassies and other places they'd never been before.

Sales jumped in the first week, but not as much as they should have. Something was wrong with our inventory accounting. We didn't make enough money in relation to what had been prepared. When the women returned and gave us the cash they'd earned, Prisca and I couldn't account for more than a third of the goods produced. My heart sank with the knowledge that women were stealing. We were putting so much goodwill into this—into them. Didn't they owe us accountability?

Not from their perspective. One woman had told us she'd sold 10 products, but by our calculations she had taken 23. She was eating a lot of doughnuts or selling them and keeping the money. I was crushed; Prisca reminded me that a number of women were being honest. The women were testing my mettle. We couldn't count on their being honest out of appreciation alone—they'd seen too many like me come and go. The existing bookkeeping system lacked accountability. No one noted how many goods each woman took in the morning.

Prisca and I crafted a simple system that would ensure accountability and reward individual behavior as well as group success. In the morning, we delivered a stern talk about how we were all in this together. If there were profits, everyone would share in them. If there were losses, everyone's pay would be reduced. The women would be paid a base wage and earn a commission on sales. The success of this venture would become the responsibility of the women themselves.

We still had work to do in breaking the charitable-project mentality. Every Friday we gathered for a pep talk. Often I would ask the women to play roles. "Consolata, I'm sitting next to you on the minibus, feeling hungry. Can you sell me something before I get off the bus?" When Prisca translated, the room erupted with giggles. Prisca smiled her oh-poor-you-who-have-so-much-to-learn smile. "Why?" I asked. "Because women do not just ask strangers to buy things on buses," she said with an air of exasperation. "Why not?" The women burst out laughing again. Prisca explained, "Because it is not polite"—a euphemism for "it is not done here."

Prisca said softly, "Jacqueline, women won't talk to someone they don't know. You have to accept it." Jacqueline said "I just want to give the women a chance." "I understand you," Prisca said, "but change is slow here. You have to give the women time."

"OK, watch this," I said. Grabbing a bucket filled with little doughnuts and waffles and *samosas*, I marched up to the street. Standing out front, I talked to the people passing by and in no time sold 10 doughnuts, more than some women sold all day. Then I marched back into the room. The women clapped and laughed. Prisca held her face in her hands and shook her head. "Jacqueline, no one will say no to a tall American girl selling them things on the streets of Nyamirambo!"

To increase sales, I ran competitions to see who could sell the most (no one would participate). I held training sessions on how to treat customers. I continued the pep talks every Friday and reminded the women that we were going to create a real bakery. Prisca would translate and the women would smile patiently and sales began to improve. Finally, something was working.

Within several months, the project was profitable. The women began to see—for the first time in their lives—a correlation between the effort they put into work and the income they earned. They began to believe the organization could succeed and that they would play a key part in that success.

Still, for every two steps forward, there was often one back. One afternoon, I received a call from a friend who had expected the women to deliver an order for a party; nothing had arrived. Prisca informed me that none of the women on duty had shown up. We learned they'd all gone to the funeral of a friend. That Friday, we called a meeting. We talked about promises made and kept. "We're not telling you not to go to the funeral," Prisca told the women, "but there are enough of us here that you can find a replacement if you can't work. This is *your* business."

One morning I walked into the offices at UNICEF and was told by a frantic office assistant that "everyone in the city is suffering from eating the baked goods." "What do you mean by 'suffering'?" I asked. "You know," he said, "they are having pains in their stomach."

I approached the women cooking. "Everyone is sick with the runs," I said. "Did you do anything differently?" They shook their heads. I asked to see what they were preparing. The smell was stale, sour, rancid. "When did you last change the cooking oil?" I asked. "Oh, never," Josepha answered gleefully. "We have been adding just a little more each day. We are keeping costs low so we can have more profit." Next lesson: quality control.

Despite the bumps, within a few months we had cornered the snack market in Kigali, expanding beyond fried dough.

I still did too much of the marketing, but in time the women gained the confidence to venture into stores to replenish orders. Within eight months, the women were earning $2 a day. Few people earned that kind of money in Rwanda, certainly not women. For the first time, their incomes allowed them to decide when to say yes and no. Despite the failures and setbacks, the little bakery continued to flourish under Prisca's leadership. It operated for a long time—until the genocide destroyed so much of what was beautiful.

The story of the bakery was the transformation that comes with being seen, held accountable, succeeding. Women acquire a sense of dignity once they were given tools for self-sufficiency. I discovered the power of creating a business with real accountability. I learned to listen with my heart and not just my head.

CHAPTER 7

The Significance of Stakeholders in Social Enterprises

Caroline Wigren-Kristoferson

**Sten K. Johnson Centre for Entrepreneurship,
Lund University**

Introduction

In this exercise, you will prepare pitches for different stakeholders. Presenting or pitching an idea is an important role of the entrepreneur. It is important to notice that as an entrepreneur one does not only need one pitch; the pitch needs to be adapted to the specific audience. This is true for all entrepreneurs, but maybe even more important for the social entrepreneur as many social enterprises are organized as hybrid organizations, that is, one part of the organization builds on charity and/or donations and has a strong social mission, while the other part works in line with a for-profit logic. This hybridity needs to be dealt with, for example by being aware about the need for different pitches. In this exercise, you train to pitch for different stakeholders, that is, different audiences. The exercise helps you to think through what to focus on depending on the audience of the pitch. By working with this exercise, you create awareness of the different stakeholders the social enterprise interacts with. You also learn to plan different pitches. However, it is important to keep in mind that there needs to be a "grand story" or "grand pitch" of the social enterprise; if the different pitches vary too much, this will lead to confusion and lack of trustworthiness. In this exercise, you will prepare in groups for presentations in class. In class, all groups will convene to discuss, debate, and defend their positions, ideas, and preferences.

Purpose/Learning Objectives

- Stakeholder theory
- The role of constructing different stories and pitches to tell about the social organization/venture for different audiences

Group Size

- Any number of groups of preferably seven members in each, but as few as four if necessary

Time Required

- One class session of 125 minutes (plus prework and longer discussion or debriefing if desired) but a minimum of 70 minutes if Introduction and Background are assigned as homework and there is no final lecture

Exercise Schedule

- The students need to have two days for preparing themselves; the exercise could be done within a shorter time period but then it is hard to expect that they develop well-thought through pitches and "grand stories." If the exercise is conducted within a shorter time frame, it could be wise to invite a founder of a social enterprise and use the guest lecture as the "grand story" and let the students develop pitches for different stakeholders.

Assignment

There are four steps to this exercise.

1. Prework

- The instructor will form groups and introduce the exercise.
- Introduce the stakeholder perspective and Burke's pentad for the students.
- There are two different ways to work with the exercise. Either, the groups are working with their own social enterprises, if they for example have as part of the course or program to plan for a social enterprise. Or, the students chose an existing social enterprise. Either or, the group must together agree on the "grand story" of the social enterprise, based on the idea, social mission to solve or contribute to, location, customers/users, stakeholders, and so on. Having done this, it is possible to start to work with how pitches can be developed for different stakeholders.
- The students should individually read Background on Stakeholders.

Background on Stakeholders

Social entrepreneurs are defined as those entrepreneurs who are not primarily striving toward economic ends. Furthermore, their initiatives are aiming at improving what is missing or does not work in public structures; they try to find new and innovative solutions in order to create an economically, socially, and ecologically sustainable society. The social entrepreneur can take action by establishing a social enterprise. Those can be seen "as a businesslike contrast to the traditional nonprofit organization" (Dart 2004). Social enterprises can be explained as organizations that employ business thinking to comply with a motive to contribute to a betterment of society rather than creating financial gain to the organization as such (or its owners) (e.g., Mair and Martí 2006; Martin and Osberg 2007; Sharir and Lerner 2006; Thompson Alvy and Lees 2000; Yujuico 2008). The social entrepreneur can also take action by establishing a nonprofit organization, or a project aiming at solving a specific issue.

There are a lot of similarities between social entrepreneurs and more traditional commercial entrepreneurs, but there are also differences. If we apply an open-system perspective on organizations, the organization is embedded in a context and it is influencing this context, but also influenced by the context. There is a constant interaction between the organization and its environment. Further, the organization, or enterprise, has different stakeholders having interests or concerns in the organization or enterprise, and the organization or enterprise have responsibilities to stakeholder groups (Freeman and Reed 1983). Stakeholders are defined as: "Any identifiable group or individual who can affect the achievement of an organization's objectives, or who is affected by the achievement of an organization's objectives" (Freeman and Reed 1983). Examples of key stakeholders are employees, customers, government (and its agencies), owners (shareholders), suppliers, unions, and the community from which the organization or enterprise draws its resources. For an organization, all stakeholders are not equally important. Both commercial entrepreneurs and social entrepreneurs have to take stakeholders into consideration. What is worth reflecting upon is that different stakeholders have different interests in the organization or enterprise.

From research, we also know that it is important for entrepreneurs to learn to "pitch" their ideas. To "pitch" is actually the same as to tell a story. The entrepreneur "pitches" to different stakeholders and the "pitches" need to be adapted to the audience. According to Lounsbury and Glynn (2001), a story is an account that legitimates the individual entrepreneur when approaching stakeholders. This is important as most new organizations or ventures do lack legitimacy. A well-constructed and told story can reduce uncertainty and create legitimacy. It is important for entrepreneurs to be aware that it is of importance to construct different stories for the different stakeholder groups.

A model that can assist when planning, writing, and telling stories of the social enterprise is Burke's pentad (agent, act, agency, purpose, and scene). Depending on who you are, which stakeholder is put in the middle, and play—the drama for the message might look different. Burke's (1962) theory on interaction and communication is constructed according to a dramatistic pentad, containing five elements and questions, which all refer to a drama (see Figure 7.1). The pentad constitutes the main figure in Burke's dramatistic method, in which the theater is rather more synonymous with life than a metaphor for life.

Act answers *what is done*, agent *who does it*, purpose *why is it done*, agency *with what means is it done*, and scene *where is it done*. The pentad

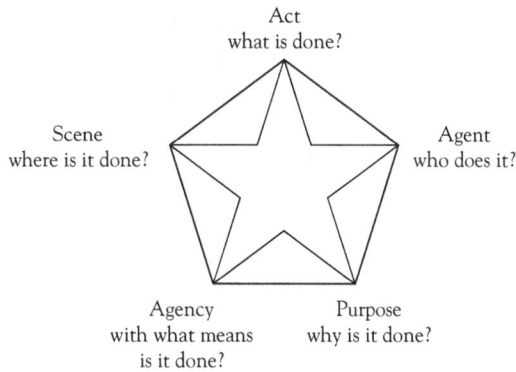

Figure 7.1 Burke's pentad

Source: Burke (1962).

gives us an opportunity to structure different types of stories. By taking the five components of the pentad into account, we get a structure for the stories to tell. According to Burke, it is important for the story to be consistent to be comprehensible. Because if it is inconsistent, it often causes confusion, irritation, doubt, and so forth. As Schwartz (1997) states in her study of how companies adjusted according to environmental demands, a case that involved Volvo, there would not exist a story of a company that manufactures cars if the story does not include assembling (action) of cars, assemblers (actors), a factory (the scene), material, machines or tools (means), and a cause (purpose) for manufacturing cars.

But, let us return to the previous discussion on stakeholders; different stakeholders have different aims and different relations to the social organization or enterprise. Table 7.1 lists a number of different stakeholders (those are only some), what each group of stakeholder does, and why they do it.

Process Instructions

Each group should prepare the "grand story" of the social enterprise, and also choose three different stakeholders for whom they develop pitches. When preparing the pitches, use the pentad by Burke. Reflect in the group about the similarities and differences between the different pitches, and between the pitches and the "grand story."

When coming to class, one group is presenting its pitches. First, they tell the "grand story" of the social enterprise, and then they pitch. The other groups of students are taking on the role as stakeholders, and are giving feedback to the students that are pitching.

In a follow-up discussion, the similarities and differences between the different pitches and between the pitches and the "grand story" of the social enterprise are evaluated. Questions to ask are: Are there too big discrepancies between the different pitches and between the pitches and the "grand story" or have the group of students managed? What could be taken into consideration to improve the pitches?

Post-work

To be able to do this exercise, the group has to prepare the "grand story" of the social enterprise before class, and the different pitches. (See Table 7.1.)

From Table 7.1, it becomes clear that the stakeholders expect different things from the social organization/enterprise. This is something the social entrepreneur needs to be aware about when constructing the story (or stories) of the organization or venture.

When constructing stories for different stakeholders, it is valuable to do it in line with Burke's pentad to find out if the story has to be revised for the different groups or not. However, it is important to remember that the different stories cannot differ too much. In the end, there must be consistency for the stories to be comprehensible. This assignment is important as it shows the role of stories—but foremost that stories must be adapted to the audience—at the same time as the social entrepreneur must show consistency in the stories told.

2. Prepare for group discussion

One group is invited to present their social venture and the "grand story" of the social venture; having done that, they are asked to present which stakeholders they have prepared pitches for, and they should do those pitches in front of class.

3. Conduct group discussion

The students in class, belonging to other groups take on the roles as different stakeholders, and they give feedback from their perspective as a

Table 7.1 Possible stakeholders to prepare pitches for

Stakeholder roles	What do they do?	Why do they do it?	How will you influence or persuade?
Founder	Invest resources in the organization/enterprise to get a salary and/or social impact from the business	To get a salary and/or for betterment of society	
Employees	Give in time and effort to make the enterprise successful	Job security, job satisfaction, and a satisfactory level of payment for their efforts	
Volunteers	Give in time and effort to make the organization successful	Betterment of society, social impact	
Users/ Consumers	People who use of buy the goods and services of the organization or enterprise	Safe and reliable products/services, value for money	
Government	Manages the economy and are responsible for legal and social issues	According to the law and politicians, they are assigned certain responsibilities	
The community	All the people who are directly or indirectly affected by the actions of the organization/ enterprise	They expect more jobs, environmental protection, socially responsible products and actions of the business, betterment of society	
Investors	Invest money and resources in the organization/enterprise	They expect some kind of return on investments; could be financial, could be social impact	

stakeholder. After each presentation and feedback round, there should be a general discussion if the "grand story" and the pitches are reasonably coherent. It could also be discussed if the group has been working in line with Burke's pentad or not. It is important to remember that the different stories cannot differ too much. In the end, there must be consistency for the stories to be comprehensible. This assignment is important as it shows the role of stories—but foremost that stories must be adapted to the audience—at the same time as the social entrepreneur must show consistency in the stories told.

4. Class discussion and debriefing

Wrap up comments and questions for class discussion.

1. What did you learn from the exercise?
2. It is necessary to develop different pitches for different stakeholders: why, why not?
3. Was it difficult to revise the pitches: why, why not?

References and Additional Resources

Burke, K. 1962. *A Grammar of Motives, and a Rhetoric of Motives.* Cleveland: World Publishing Company.

Dart, R. 2004. "The Legitimacy of Social Enterprise." *Nonprofit Management and Leadership* 14, no. 4, pp. 411–424.

Freeman, R.E., and D.L. Reed. 1983. "Stockholders and Stakeholders: A New Perspective on Corporate Governance." *California Management Review* 25, no. 3, pp. 88–106.

Mair, J., and I. Martí. 2006. "Social Entrepreneurship Research: A Source of Explanation, Prediction, and Delight." *Journal of World Business* 41, no. 1, pp. 36–44.

Martin, R.L., and S. Osberg. 2007. "Social Entrepreneurship: The Case for Definition." *Stanford Social Innovation Review* (Spring) 5, no. 2, pp. 29–39.

Sharir, M., and M. Lerner. 2006. "Gauging the Success of Social Ventures Initiated by Individual Social Entrepreneurs." *Journal of World Business* 41, no. 1, pp. 6–20.

Thompson, J., G. Alvy, and A. Lees. 2000. "Social Entrepreneurship: A New Look at the People and the Potential." *Management Decision* 38, no. 5, pp. 328–338.

Yujuico, E. 2008. "Connecting the Dots in Social Entrepreneurship Through the Capabilities Approach." *Socio-Economic Review* 6, no. 3, pp. 493–513.

CHAPTER 8

Creating Social Value

Alia Weston

OCAD University (Toronto)

Introduction

In many societies, economic decline has had detrimental effects on society, and has left communities in need of regeneration (Thompson, Alvy, and Lees 2000). Social entrepreneurs often work within contexts such as these, and are focused on creating business that are aimed at solving challenges faced by communities, or society at large. In doing so, they generate value for society by contributing to the well-being of a community (Imas and Weston 2016; Peredo and McLean 2006). In addition to the need for regeneration, economic decline also has an impact on the availability of resources. Previously abundant resources may become limited or cease to be available altogether. As a result, social entrepreneurs often have to be resourceful and repurpose whatever limited or discarded resources they have around them (Zahra et al. 2009; Di Domenico et al. 2010). In this way, they essentially *create* or *make* their own resources by using their limitations to their advantage.

Following these perspectives, this exercise explores how value can be practically *created* or *made* for society with the use of limited or discarded resources. In the exercise, students will work through an activity to understand how it feels to practically engage with limited amounts of discarded materials, as well as the creative and improvisational engagement that is required to overcome limitations. Participants will work together in groups to complete the activity and will then come together after the activity to analyze their learning from the experience. The primary outcomes of the exercise are for students to understand what it feels like to *create* or *make* an idea that is valuable or useful to society, and at the same time work with materials that are not abundant, or repurposing those that appear to be useless. In addition, another important aspect of the exercise is the critical examination of the role that practical creation (i.e., physical making of artifacts) has in facilitating this understanding.

The ultimate objective of this exercise is to direct students to think more deeply and challenge their preconceived ideas that they may have about a subject. In this exercise, the challenge is to think more deeply about the meaning of social entrepreneurship, and the ways that social problems are solved despite the limited availability of resources. However, the exercise can be adapted to challenge students thinking about related topics such as social entrepreneurship, creativity, or (social) innovation.

Purpose/Learning Objectives

The learning objectives for this exercise are to:

- To develop an idea for a social enterprise, a business that solves a social problem, by using limited materials as inspiration.
- To critically examine how social entrepreneurs create value for society (e.g., addressing social problems) by (re)using the materials they have around them.
- To critically examine the practical experience of working with limited resources, as well as the improvisational engagement required overcome limitations.
- There are two key takeaways from this exercise. The first is the ability of participants to come up with an idea that is valuable or useful to society using repurposed materials. The second is the critical examination of the role that practical creation has on facilitating understanding.

Group Size

This exercise works well with a class size between 6 to 30 participants. Group size should ideally be between 2 to 5 participants.

Time Required

One class session of 100 minutes is required for the full activity. Discussion or debriefing times can be adjusted as required, but a minimum of 70 minutes is needed to complete the activity.

Exercise Schedule and Activities

There are two steps to this exercise.

1. Pre-Activity

    Readings: Based on the class type or level, students can be assigned readings from the "References and Readings" section. The instructor should determine which readings and how many to assign. Students should read the articles individually before the class.

    Materials: A primary part of the activity is the repurposing of discarded materials; therefore materials should be prepared before the exercise is run. Example materials include any discarded materials that could be incorporated into a craft activity, for example, plastic bags; old paper/magazines/newspaper/card; coffee cups; soft plastic containers; discarded packaging from groceries or food. Please note that it is best for the all discarded materials should be clean and easy to break/tear or cut.

    - Option 1—Facilitator collects materials. The facilitator collects a store of "discarded materials" before the activity is run. This is the best option if there are time constraints, or if a materials theme is incorporated. The facilitator should also collect "extra materials," which participants can use to aid their making process, for example, the scissors, tape, or glue.
    - Option 2—Participants collect materials. The facilitator may choose to ask participants to collect materials that have been discarded in their own communities, or materials that they have discard themselves. This option is effective for facilitating a greater connection between the students and the materials they may (re)use in their own lives. Note that

if Option 2 is taken, the facilitator should factor in the time required and collect some materials as a back-up.

2. Group Exercise

The schedule for the group activity is outlined as follows. The schedule is approximate and based on the 100 minutes, but times can be adjusted as required. The instructor will form groups in class on the day of the activity.

Activity	Materials	Time (mins)
Introduction Introduction to the exercise, explanation of the exercise format, and group formation.	Power Point	10
Pre-Exercise Reflection Participants should individually write down thoughts: • What is entrepreneurship? • What is social entrepreneurship? • Pardons are the motivations and inspirations of social entrepreneurs? • Can social enterprises be developed with minimal resources?	Scrap paper	10
Practical Activity: Making a Social Enterprise Participants will be divided into groups of 2 to 5 and given the brief: • Each group should use whatever materials the participants have with them on the day, AND/OR the groups can be given a small amount of discarded materials by the facilitator. • Each group should create a social enterprise. In other words, they should come up with an idea for a business that solves a social problem and creates value for society, or their immediate community. They should develop an idea and practically make it using the discarded materials as inspiration. • The facilitator will regulate the availability of materials while groups are working (*see following explanation). • Following the activity, each group will present their social enterprise idea, as well as any props or materials they have produced, to the other groups.	Whatever materials the participants have with them on the day, AND/OR The discarded materials provided by the facilitator (e.g., scrap paper, paper cups, newspaper, plastic bags, etc.)	40

(Continued)

Activity	Materials	Time (mins)
* Regulation of Resources by Facilitator While the workshop is taking place, the facilitator should regulate materials without warning so that participants feel the effect of their resources being limited. The facilitator can choose to give a group extra materials that will help them (e.g., the scissors, tape or glue etc.) to aid their idea creation, but should also take materials away without warning. The aim of the regulation is to allow the participants the feel what it is like to work with limited resources. They will experience the feeling of resources taken away while they are depending on them, as well as the feeling of unexpectedly improvising and using resources when they do become available. If time permits, the facilitator can also choose to unexpectedly extend or limit the time that participants have to complete the activity.	Materials to aid production (e.g., scissors, tape, or glue, etc.)	
Judging Following the activity, each group's social enterprise idea or products will be judged by the other groups. The basic criteria for judging is as follows: • Does the social enterprise successfully create value for society? Would the other groups realistically use the products or services being offered the social enterprise if they were available to the public?	Power Point	15
Post-Activity Reflection and Debate The class should discuss their insights about their experience of undertaking the exercise and relate their thoughts back to the theoretical/ topics concepts presented at the start of the exercise (10 mins). If time permits before the class discussion, participants can individually note down their thoughts about their experience (10 mins). The following questions are examples that can be used to guide refection and a full group discussion.	Scrap paper	20

(*Continued*)

Activity	Materials	Time (mins)
Questions about the activity and practical creation-making: • How easy or difficult was the task? • What did it feel like to have to physically produce something that is of value to society with limited materials? • What was your experience of using the materials around you? How did you improvise to overcome limitations? • Did your physical engagement with the materials make you think differently about the theory or meaning of social entrepreneurship? • Following this activity, do you think it possible for social enterprises to create value for society by using limited materials? What are the opportunities and limitations? *Questions for individuals about real-world implications:* • How can you personally be more conscious about the ways in which you make use of resources in your work and life? • In what ways can you do more with less and repurpose what you have around you to create value for society? In what ways can you be more improvisational when you are *repurposing* materials in your work and lives?		
Critical Debate	Participants should discuss the activity and their reflections following guiding questions: • What can be produced with limited resources? • What are the motivations and inspirations of social entrepreneurs? • What are the implications for developing social enterprises with minimal resources?	10

(*Continued*)

Activity	Materials	Time (mins)
Concluding Points and Round-Up The learning objectives of the exercise should be reemphasized at the end of the activity. For example: • A social entrepreneur does not require many (or expensive) resources to successfully solve social problems. • Social entrepreneurs can successful generate value for society by repurposing whatever materials they have around them. • This exercise is about more than simply recycling waste materials; it is about thinking about the ways that change can be made when people repurpose the limited or discarded material they have around them. Gaining insight from the practical engagement with materials is a valuable way of enabling deep thinking about theoretical concepts.	Power Point	5

References and Additional Resources

Di Domenico, M.L., H. Haugh, and P. Tracey. 2010. "Social Bricolage: Theorizing Social Value Creation in Social Enterprises." *Entrepreneurship Theory and Practice* 34, no. 4, pp. 681–703.

Imas, J.M., and A. Weston. 2016. "Organsparkz Communities of Art/creative Spaces, Imaginations, & Resistance." In *The Arts, Social & Organizational Change: Precarious Spaces,* eds. K.Kosmala and J.M. Imas. Bristol, England: Intellect Books.

Peredo, A.M., and M. McLean. 2006. "Social Entrepreneurship: A Critical Review of the Concept." *Journal of World Business* 41, no. 1, pp. 56–65.

Thompson, J., G. Alvy, and A. Lees. 2000. "Social Entrepreneurship: A New Look at the People and the Potential." *Management Decision* 38, no. 5, pp. 328–38.

Zahra, S.A., E. Gedajlovich, D.O. Neubaum, and J.M. Shulman. 2009. "A Typology of Social Entrepreneurs: Motives, Search Processes and Ethical Challenges." *Journal of Business Venturing* 25, no. 5, pp. 519–32.

CHAPTER 9

The Organizational Form Design Studio

Elizabeth A.M. Searing

University at Albany, State University of New York

Introduction

In this exercise, you will discuss and determine the appropriate organizational form for different types of social enterprise ventures. Using the knowledge from the commentaries in this workbook, you use the responses to six key questions about the venture to fit the type that gives the venture the best chances at success based on its mission, operations, and relationship with its ecosystem.

Learning Objectives

- To familiarize potential entrepreneurs with the information and decisions required to choose an appropriate corporate form.
- To move beyond the solo entrepreneur model and into the more valid team model with social goal.
- *Optional:* To develop a foundation for a semester-long project or venture launch having in mind the social entrepreneur.

Group Size

This exercise can utilize any number of groups of 3 to 5 members each. There should be enough members to encourage healthy discussion, but not enough that individual members of the group are not heard. This number also closely approximates the founding leadership or core consulting team.

Time Required

About 60 to 75 minutes, depending on length of discussions. The discussion can be broken into two sessions, depending on normal session or class length. Reading of previous chapters and preparation for the exercise should ideally be conducted prior to class in order to maximize the usefulness of the time available for interaction, but such reading (or supplementary reading on corporate forms) can be conducted in class as part of a two- or three-session experience. If there are any questions regarding the selection of appropriate pre-class reading materials, please check with your facilitator or instructor. If you are engaging in self-directed study, please read the chapters in this workbook on corporate form, plus the recommended readings included at the end of this exercise.

Exercise Schedule

Following reading preparation, this exercise has four major sections. The first two discuss the more limited case study included in this chapter, with discussion occurring at the more interactive small group level before the group advocates as part of a larger class discussion. The third and fourth sections follow the same pattern using the more open-ended sample case included in this exercise. If necessary, additional time can be added to the beginning of the exercise for in-class reading of the material.

	Unit time	Total time
1. Group Discussion of the Case Study	10 min	10 min
2. Class Discussion of the Case Study	10 min	20 min
3. Group Discussion of the Sample Case	20 min	40 min
4. Class Discussion on the Sample Case	20 min	60 min

Assignment

1. Background and preparation

   As you will have noticed in your readings, there is a wide variety of organizational forms available to your social venture. In *The Social Enterprise Zoo* (Young, Brewer, and Searing 2016), the editors encourage readers to view the many different types of social enterprise like the animals in a zoological park or nature preserve. Variety in both animal type and how they are grouped is encouraged, but you need to keep in mind certain characteristics if you're going to keep the "animals" healthy. For example, homeless shelters are often dependent on government grants and donative support with little competition from other ventures; like pandas, they subsist on a very particular diet and require a heavily structured environment to protect the species. Meanwhile, the hospital sector has a variety of forms and heavy competition—this is more akin to the increased competition between polar bears and grizzlies in North America. This situation is particularly apt for two reasons. First, even though these species exist in the wild, the impact of man-made global warming has altered their ecosystem and driven the conflict. Thus, the analogy is not limited to the old-fashioned Victorian notion of a zoo. Second, the increased competition for resources has caused hybridization between the two bear species to occur—much like the corporate form speciation occurring around the world for social ventures.

In the United States, such forms are determined by several different parts of the government. For example, what is commonly referred to as a "nonprofit" is a designated tax exemption granted by the federal Internal Revenue Service. A limited liability corporation can be found in all 50 states, but are guided by different statutes within each state. And benefit corporations (one of the new corporate forms) are not yet found in every state, plus can have substantial differences between states that recognize them since each state designs its own definition.

On an international level, the picture is even more complex. For example, Europe has a much more robust cooperative sector than the United States, so the likelihood that a social venture may be a cooperative is higher. Further, many countries within Europe have social venture forms and definitions of charities unique to their country. When completing this exercise, you should feel free to adapt the discussion to the context most relevant to your social venture's operation. Be mindful that this question will become more complicated if your social venture intends to operate in two different environments, whether across states or across countries.

2. Determinants of organizational form

Since social ventures exist in a variety of different corporate forms, choosing between them can be an intimidating challenge for the entrepreneur. Social ventures can be for-profit, nonprofit, low-profit, or a combination of different types. Each of these types can live in a broad variety of environments and ecosystems, though they may thrive in only a few. There are six factors that describe your potential social venture that are essential in deciding what environment it needs to achieve its full impact. Either on your own or at the beginning of the session (check with your instructor or facilitator), consider the following questions in determining the best fit.

What are the social venture's purpose and/or mission? The social nature of the venture is what separates social entrepreneurs from other entrepreneurs. A clear understanding and commitment to this mission is critical, especially in decisions where profit maximization with and without mission pursuit are divergent.

What does the social venture do? This is a separate question from the venture's purpose. For example, even though TOMS Shoes' mission was originally to address the hardships caused by an absence of shoes in children struggling with poverty, the venture does so by selling its own line of shoes in the commercial market and donating a pair of shoes for each sold at market price (TOMS Shoes 2006). The operations of shoe manufacture are very different than the operations of shoe donation, but both are core to the venture.

What resources does the social venture consume? Is the venture more dependent on a particular resource, like the panda? Though many social ventures are driven primarily by market exchange, this is not necessarily the case. Even if it is, there may be several different markets or groups of potential customers within markets that should be considered separately with their own unique cultivation and development needs.

Where does this social venture live? As mentioned previously, the location of the social venture (or the location of its incorporation, if different from the physical location) plays a large part in the availability and appropriateness of the corporate form choice. This is an especially important question in two situations. The first is when the mission recipients are different from the market recipients. Where the venture is located relative to both of these groups will play a large role in determining operations and, thus, the venture's form. The second is when the venture will operate across jurisdictional lines, whether across countries or across states. A social entrepreneur needs to be aware of the regulations and norms of all locations that not only their venture, but also representation of their venture, may appear.

How does this social venture interact with other organizations? There are two facets to this question. The first is on a personal level. The depth and breadth of the social and business networks of the founding team are crucially important in the success of a venture. If the founding entrepreneurs have a large network of amicable connections and partnerships, these will likely extend to the start-up. The second level of interaction is on an organizational level: are there several competitors in the venture's space, or in closely related spaces? What are the opportunities for horizontal or vertical networking? If a venture merges or is acquired by another organization, there are certain organizational forms that can facilitate such a move. Additionally, some social ventures are two or more separate organizations from a start-up, such as a corporation with a corporate-owned private foundation or a nonprofit with a wholly-owned LLC.

What does this social venture need to do to be considered successful? Be sure and think holistically about this question. Does success include both financial and social goals? Are both able to be converted into measurable benchmarks? Are there certain stakeholders that will influence the definition of success more than others, such as a foundation grant or venture capital?

The answer(s) to each question will give insight into how different organizational form choices might thrive. Be sure and write down your responses, even just in note form, so that you can refer to them during group discussion. Since there is a limited amount of information, be sure and also explicitly state any assumptions you may be depending on: this includes market conditions, the identity and desires of stakeholders, and so on.

Analysis and Discussion

	Unit time	Total time
1. Small Group Discussion: Sample Case 1	10 min	10 min

Using your own recorded thoughts, briefly discuss each question in the interest of coming to a consensus. Try to make sure that everyone in your group is heard: remember, teams are often made of very different skills and personalities. When a consensus for each response is reached, note what the response is so that it can easily be referred to during the classroom discussion. As a final step, try to reach a consensus on the type of organizational form that is most appropriate to Case 1.

	Unit time	Total time
2. Class/Large Group Discussion: Sample Case 1	10 min	20 min

Continue the discussion of the case as a class by pooling the suggested organizational form types suggested by the Small Groups. The emphasis in the Class/Large Group discussion is on the form for the venture, with the answers to the six questions being used as supporting reasoning for the recommendation. Be sure to employ a method of recording that allows participants to retain and revisit the information later for reference. This can be either an instructor-led recording of the salient point on a white board or electronic device, or groups can nominate members to communicate the ideas of the small group either verbally or by writing responses on a white board. Consensus is not necessary at this stage, but rather an acknowledgement of the many different assumptions and possibilities that can arise from this situation.

	Unit time	Total time
3. Small Group Discussion: Sample Case 2	20 min	40 min

The second sample case is an example of a type of social enterprise that often involves a variety of ventures or networks, though not necessarily so. A large amount of additional material is available in the popular press, and this can be utilized to the extent desired by your instructor or facilitator. You and your team should be able to reference the information they rely on in addition to any assumptions which are needed to make their suggestions viable by writing their recommendation down. As with the first case, your team should be prepared to share their thoughts and findings with the other small groups.

	Unit time	Total time
4. Class/Large Group Discussion: Sample Case 2	20 min	60 min

As with the first case, your discussion of the second sample case as a large group should concentrate on the form recommendation, supported by potential issues and solutions rather than a right or wrong verdict on the suggestion. The potential that your group members may come from different states or nationalities makes this a particularly challenging and rich exercise. At the conclusion of the exercise, you should have a working understanding of how to apply your knowledge of corporate forms in a start-up situation, with this understanding broadened by the experiences and thoughts of your colleagues.

References and Additional Resources

Brewer, C.V., E.S. Minnigh, and R.A. Wexler. 2014. *Social Enterprise by Non-Profits and Hybrid Organizations.* Bloomberg BNA, No. 489-1st.

Galera, G., and C. Borzaga. 2009. "Social Enterprise: An International Overview of its Conceptual Evolution and Legal Implementation." *Social Enterprise Journal* 5, no. 3, pp. 210–228.

Kerlin, J.A. 2006. "Social Enterprise in the United States and Europe: Understanding and Learning from the Differences." *Voluntas: International Journal of Voluntary & Nonprofit Organizations* 17, no. 3, pp. 246–263.

TOMS Shoes. 2006. "About TOMS" www.toms.com/about-toms#companyInfo (accessed November 3, 2015).

Wexler, R.A. 2009. "Effective Social Enterprise: A Menu of Legal Structures," *The Exempt Organization Tax Review* 63, no. 6, pp. 565–75.

Young, D., C.V. Brewer, and E.A.M. Searing, eds. 2016. *The Social Enterprise Zoo: A Guide to Perplexed Scholars, Entrepreneurs, Philanthropists, Leaders, Investors and Policymakers.* (Cheltenham: Edward Elgar.

Organizational Form Design Studio Case 1: Urban Food Deserts

You're a long-time resident of the big city of Kurumaville, which has been slipping into hard fiscal times. Similar to other downtown areas, there are large areas where no grocery stores are available, which means that healthier and more reasonably priced foods are not accessible by the residents. The easy access to unhealthy foods is adding to a growing health problem in Kurumaville residents. You know that there are farmers' markets in the suburbs and large amounts of farmland outside of the city, so you want to find a way to connect residents of the city with the healthier foods you know are available. What are three ways you can think of that would do this? Keep in mind the six factors.

Organizational Form Design Studio Case 2: Social Enterprise Incubator

A start-up incubator helps increase the chances of a successful venture launch by providing access to colleagues, experts, and a host of other services. These are commonplace, especially at universities or targeting subsectors such as technology or bioengineering. However, there are relatively few dedicated to incubating social enterprises. Some of the early examples were Propeller in New Orleans, Pananzee in Chicago, Santa Clara University's Global Social Benefit Institute, or the worldwide ImpactHub network. Beyond grants or fellowship programs, these pioneers provide a physical location in addition to services and expertise.

Having a physical location, however, comes with additional difficulties. Sustaining a healthy social enterprise ecosystem, especially one that is robust enough to take in and cultivate groups of start-ups, takes a great deal of financial and human capital. The social enterprise incubators just mentioned have taken on a variety of different legal forms, often multiple forms joined together to provide different benefits or services.

Your challenge is to design a social enterprise incubator for your town (or, if group members are all from different towns, use the current town of the individual whose name comes last in alphabetical order). Which corporate form(s) will you use? Use the six factors as a guide, remembering that you will likely need to offer a suite of services and are required to have a physical location for entrepreneurs to share a workspace. Also be sure to keep in mind the geographical location of your incubator, since laws and corporate forms available will vary by country and state.

CHAPTER 10

Beyond the Business Case

Gary Shaheen

Social Dynamics, LLC

Summary

This case provides an example of individual entrepreneurship for people with disabilities. Social entrepreneurship's both social and economic goals can be met by seeding and supporting small-scale venture creation that assists people with disabilities to achieve financial stability and improve social inclusion. Social entrepreneurship students who understand the fundamentals of small venture development will benefit from this case. Disability studies students who understand person-centered planning and the employment challenges faced by people with disabilities are also likely to benefit from this case. The optimal benefit may be realized by assigning students of both disciplines as members of the same study teams to better leverage and apply their specific academic knowledge to the case example. After students read through the case, they will answer challenge questions related to the entrepreneur's personal, venture operational infrastructure, and environmental barriers to a new venture start-up, using an "Inclusive Entrepreneurship Template." The case exercise provides students with an opportunity to critically examine and discuss how they would assist a prospective entrepreneur with a disability in overcoming the personal, small enterprise infrastructure and environmental challenges that prospective entrepreneurs with disabilities often face in developing or scaling up their new ventures.

There are three aspects to the Inclusive Entrepreneurship Template that students will consider for the case exercise:

Individual-centric aspects: Students will explore the entrepreneur's personal background as presented in the case. They will focus upon the entrepreneur's skills and talents, motivation for starting a small venture, support networks, impacts of disabilities on a venture start-up, the perceived venture opportunity, daily life routines affecting the enterprise and other factors necessary to understanding the "owner behind the small venture." Students will critically examine and discuss the ways that disabilities can affect new venture creation both positively and negatively based upon the information provided in the case example.

Venture-centric aspects: Here is where students explore the small venture start-up infrastructure including the essential elements of the new venture plan, and its marketing plans; its product/service mix; financial accounting systems; technology; facilities and equipment; supply chain; inventory management systems; and other factors that are necessary to conduct the day-day operations of the small venture.

Context-centric aspects: New small ventures operate in a variety of contexts and environments unique to their product/services mix, operational strengths and constraints, relationship to their markets, and other factors. Students will examine how the venture proposes to interact with these environments that can also include how it positions itself in relationship to government regulations, legal issues, customers, suppliers, and other public and private agencies that interact with, and support employment and entrepreneurship for people with disabilities. Students will critically examine and better understand the venture's market niche; competitors; the economic conditions affecting the venture's operations; (including financing opportunities, networks of mentors and associations with disability support services agencies); and other factors that the small venture must consider to get its products and services produced and to the market. Students will gain a better appreciation for both the challenges and opportunities for new venture creation encountered by entrepreneurs with disabilities.

Learning Objectives

By the end of the case exercise, students will develop improved awareness and knowledge of the challenges and barriers often encountered by small ventures prospectively owned by people with disabilities that include: underdeveloped business planning skills; under-capitalization; insufficient market leveraging ability; lack of new venture infrastructure elements (that can include accounting, law, finance, marketing or advertising); lack of strong venture creation and support networks; and difficulties in negotiating environments that support new venture creation where accommodations for a person's disability may not be available.

Case Example: "Belts by John"

1. Person-centric aspects

    Background: John Jones is a 55-year-old African American man who was a former truck driver. He was forced to retire from his 25-year career due to a vehicle accident that he sustained while working, which affected his eyesight. Since he left his job two years ago, his eyesight has gotten progressively worse and he is now classified as legally blind. Where once he relished being on the road as a driver, and being able to support himself and his family, he now spends most of his days attending group activities at a Recreation Center with other people with visual disabilities, or reading books and periodicals in Braille. He learned how to produce leather crafts at his group sessions and pursues leatherworking as a hobby. Leatherworking keeps him active and gives him a purpose. He also says that it helps him to avoid the occasional bouts of depression he experiences when he thinks about the way his life used to be. He particularly misses meeting all sorts of people in his travels. It seems that now, except for his wife, everyone he associates with, also has a visual disability. He gets tired sometimes of people at the Recreation Center that can't seem to talk about anything other than their disability. And, in the community, he finds that he is often regarded with pity as a person with an apparent disability, not as the independent, skilled person he knows that he still is. As he continued to lose his eyesight, he became more and more interested in getting back to being the self-reliant person he always was, by converting his leatherworking hobby into a new venture.

    John's idea is to create a selection of hand-tooled belts, including belts that truck drivers would buy for back support. His counselor at the Commission for the Blind and Visually Handicapped (CBVH) told him that he is limited in the amount of outside income he can make without losing his Social Security benefits or affecting his Worker's Compensation benefits. CBVH is a New York State agency that helps people with visual disabilities obtain living, educational, public assistance, and employment benefits and opportunities. But the counselor also said that financial assistance for the purchase of equipment could be available if he presented them with a business plan that demonstrates the viability of the venture. CBVH could also arrange to provide benefits planning assistance, so John could use special work incentives that might allow him to make money and not lose his benefits until his income is sufficient for him to become self-sufficient. He has to remain within limits for the personal cash assets he can maintain without loss of benefits, but he does have about $2,000.00 that he has saved up that can be used to help start the new venture.

Venture Concept: Belts by John is a new start-up venture proposing to offer high-quality leather belts and accessories to people who look for genuine U.S.-made leather goods. The core attribute that Belts by John offers is its quality—they will be genuine leather belts that the customer could use for years. Through customization, the customers will be able to tailor the belt under their own preferences. For example, for the truck driver, the unique value that Belts by John provides is the stability it can provide to the lower back for extended periods of time that is directly related to the high quality of the belt.

He is also aware of some of the challenges in creating his new venture—particularly how a person with a visual disability could achieve production benchmarks using machinery that was created for use by people with good vision. His new venture proposes to generate revenues through selling belts, but also by inspiring others with his type of disability by potentially teaching leatherworking techniques to other people who are blind. John does not know what the market rate for a belt similar to those he would produce would be, but he estimates the retail price of a regular everyday belt to be about $50. He does not know how he would market his belts, but he hopes to sell the belts through online belt shops and handcraft shops. He estimates that he can produce 3 to 4 belts per day using his hand tools. But he also knows that cutting, punching, sewing, and tooling machinery exists that will dramatically increase his daily production. He does not know if the equipment would allow operation by a person who is blind.

Venture Opportunity: According to John, the new venture opportunity is generated by his perception that the public and specialized segments like truck drivers need high-quality belts for safety, status, and for daily use. He has not undertaken any formal marketing research to substantiate these assumptions. However, he has contacted people he knows in the trucking industry and was told that high-quality driver's belts could be a saleable commodity to individuals and companies. He also polled people at the Recreation Center on three different occasions about their interest in buying quality leather belts and received generally favorable responses. He does not yet know when customers would choose his belt over those of competitors. He has sold 15 belts during the past year that he made by hand over a 6-week period to friends and family at an average price of $35 each.

2. Venture-centric aspects

New Venture Infrastructure: John needs a strong business and operational plan in order to realize his hopes for a financially viable small venture. As the new venture is still in its developmental stage, there are currently no existing financial records of past sales, nor is there a point of sale system in place. His accounting systems are not in place that might enable him to determine the company's breakeven point. John wants to sell his belts for $50 each and estimates that the production cost per unit is approximately $20 to $25. He buys his raw leather in small quantities through a local wholesaler, but has not explored if he could purchase at a greater discount if he bought leather in quantity. He works from a room in his home, so storage space is small, although he plans to move his operations to his large basement. These factors would necessarily be included in his business plan that would allow him to apply for the CBVH start-up capital.

Belts by John also need to formulate a system for receiving and processing payments for its products. John needs to be able to process credit cards, cash, and potentially payments for large orders. He will also have to pay suppliers for inventory and potentially for machinery upkeep, a process that will require significant planning. Once the new venture is more mature, the company will need budgeting plans to ensure that John always has enough funds available to purchase necessary inventory and potential equipment maintenance. He also needs a system that tracks sales on a commission basis.

Operations: At this stage, John has not made a specific decision about the styles of product that he will offer. Instead, he wants to create a customized product where customers can select the belt's hide, color, and their own design. Formalizing a basic design frame that can be customized could simplify production and inventory management. The beginning process of making belts, such as dyeing and drying hide, generally involves considerable time. However, he expects that most of his final work will be done by machines and will take less than half an hour to finish.

John works at leather goods production now when he feels like it. He thinks that by improving a work-flow calendar, he will be able to develop other aspects of the new venture during each queue time as belts are being stamped and sized. For example, he might expand his new venture to include book covers, key chains, and wallets to maximize the usage of hide and use up scrap. John wants to market the products in local custom leather stores, boutiques, and online distributors. Since managing a website regularly requires professional managing skills, he plans to outsource the online sales to a third party. After receiving an order, he plans to use United State Postal Services (USPS) as his preferred shipping method to deliver the product with flat rate boxes from home. He chose USPS because first class rates include insurance of up to $50 per box and free delivery tracking.

Equipment and Production: John's new venture needs a sound infrastructure before operations can begin. He plans to order all of the machinery and equipment needed to start his new venture from a leatherworking catalogue. But he is not sure that they can be used by a person who is blind, so he needs to do more research. At first, he will order just enough materials to start his new venture and produce up to 12 belts per week. As his products become recognized and the demand for his belts grow, then John will explore getting a bulk discount on his supplies. Depending on his new venture plan, John could receive his machinery and initial materials at no cost through CBVH funding, which will significantly reduce start-up costs. But they will not release funds until he presents them with a viable new venture plan. CBVH also needs to know if a machine John selects can be used safely by a person who is blind.

John also needs to renovate his basement, which he estimates to be under $1000 in cost as his stepson is completing all aspects of the improvement for free. His basement has approximately 400 square feet of space that he can use for production and storage. As of now, John's basement will likely be sufficient for his production levels but there should be a plan in place should production volumes exceed the space available. The company will not likely need any additional full-time employees immediately but again, there needs to be a plan in place should the company's sales grow quickly.

John currently has a computer that he uses somewhat frequently but he thinks that he may want to buy a laptop before he begins the new venture. This potential cost needs to be included in the company's internal infrastructure needs, should the purchase be made. If the company's equipment ever breaks down, John will need to have enough money available to pay for moderate repairs to machinery. Finally, John needs to keep records of the products he produces in addition to his financial records.

3. Context-centric aspects

Market Assumptions: The potential target market of Belts by John are people who look for quality custom-made leather belts, western style attire, the motorcycle enthusiast, as well as truck drivers that will use them for safety purposes. John does not yet know if his market assumptions are correct, but he thinks he will need two types of marketing research: primary market research and secondary market research. Through primary research, he thinks that conducting a customer survey will help him understand if the customers are interested in his product, the price they would be willing to pay, and what else John could do to improve the product and its market position. From secondary industry research, he will know what type of customer will be mostly interested in genuine leather goods.

Branding and Market Positioning: In order to increase recognition of his brand, John wants to craft a story about his entrepreneurial spirit as a person who is blind. Along with the inspiring story, Belts by John will be seen as more than another leather brand marketed to customers. Instead, buying the leather goods becomes another way of demonstrating that people with disabilities can contribute to the economy as new venture owners and earn real wages when they can start and own their own new ventures.

Distribution: Since it is hard for John to take care of product development, production, and operation by himself, he thinks that he should sell the product through third-party distributors such as online stores and leather goods wholesalers. He thinks that different distribution strategies should be designed to reach out to different types of customers. For instance, safety belts for truck drivers could be distributed through wholesalers that could sell to trucking companies.

Competitive Environment: John believes he will face a large number of direct and indirect competitive threats. Direct competitors will be the local leather shops, and online stores that focus on leather products. Also, there is product overlap with major retailers like the U.S.-based firms J.C. Penney, Macy's, and Target, particularly for belts, that will be another competitive risk for his new venture. He believes that sustaining high-quality products and understanding customer's trends will be the solution to overcome the potential threats.

Financing: John wants to obtain funding from CBVH. CVBH can provide up to $10,000 to aid in new venture start-ups, including equipment based on a feasibility analysis and a commercially viable new venture plan. If funding is granted, then CBVH will purchase the machines for John, so they don't show up as an asset and affect the receipt of his disability benefits. John also has to prove that the new venture will earn him living wage income over time, and is not a just a hobby used to make a little extra money. He needs to be earning at least minimum wage from the sales of his products. John thinks that once he gets over the learning curve, he'll be able to make more than minimum wage. But in the short term, he estimates that his owner's draw will be equal to federal minimum wage.

Networks: John's support team consists of his new venture partner Bill White and his CBVH counselor, Dennis Kitchen. Dennis, along with other CBVH employees, will actually be responsible for approving John's final new venture plan so John must be in constant communication with them as he develops his venture. Bill is a very close friend of John and will help with certain tasks that may be difficult for him to complete. Bill took financial literacy and Quick-Books training, so he will be able to help with the early stages of the company's financials. He can assist John in shipping, bookkeeping, and so on, and he has also been doing a lot of reading for John while Dennis finalizes the purchase of a portable reader. Bill has sufficient ability in using Microsoft Excel to assist John in maintaining financial records. John has relationships with people from a couple of different new venture incubators in the area as well. He has been told that he may be able to rent incubator space, once his new venture gets started. His social networks, once large, have diminished greatly since he became disabled and his ability to get around has been compromised since he can't drive a car.

Despite his challenges, John believes that he has the skills and determination and the knowledge needed to become a successful entrepreneur. He also hopes that once his new venture is established, he can create jobs for other people with disabilities.

Assignment

1. Prework
   Prework includes developing a working familiarity with the Inclusive Entrepreneurship Template, described in the following. Students also will view a video "*Aimee Mullins and Her 10 Pairs of Legs*" (www. ted.com/talks/aimee_mullins_prosthetic_aesthetics.html), which challenges popular conceptions of disability as meaning "non-abled."

Students will also be introduced to additional resources on the topic that include readings from the syllabus on topics related to social inclusion of people with disabilities, the meaning and context of entrepreneurship, and practical methods for supporting entrepreneurship for people with disabilities. The brief vignettes of successful new ventures started by entrepreneurs with disabilities contained in Griffin and Hammis' "Making Self-Employment Work for People with Disabilities" (Griffin and Hammis 2003) offer additional evidence that disability labels need not be an impediment to success as an entrepreneur. Orienting students to strengths-based concepts concerning people with disabilities will help in establishing a framework for them to better understand not only the challenges, but also the strengths that can arise from living with a disability and become a potential resource as they create new ventures.

2. Postwork

After intensive classwork, discussion concludes, and students are expected to think about and apply their insights and their knowledge to challenge questions in their work as social entrepreneurs helping to create small ventures that are owned and operated by people with diverse disabilities.

Theoretical Framework

"Entrepreneurs are innovative, opportunity-oriented, resourceful, value-creating change agents" (Dees, Emerson, and Economy 2001). These change agents can operate in the for-profit, commercial sector creating product innovations for commercial purposes (Steve Jobs of Apple Corporation, for example), or in the social, nonprofit sector, realigning systems and creating new opportunities for blended business and social impact. While commercial enterprises may adopt social goals by establishing philanthropic divisions within their corporations, the company's primary *raison d'etre* is commercial, not social return on investment. However, as Dees et al. note, social entrepreneurs are different than commercial entrepreneurs since they start out with a social purpose in mind and apply business methods to achieve a goal of positive social change. The return on investment is measured by the level of achievement of the social purpose as well as the level of success of their business methods.

Much of the research on the topic of social entrepreneurship examines social ventures that are created to involve groups of individuals with disabilities and/or disadvantages with the goal of equalizing their participation in the labor force and helping them achieve financial stability commensurate with their nondisabled peers (Dees and Economy 2001; Defourney and Nyssens 2007; Roberts Economic Development Fund 2015; Warner and Mandiberg 2006). However, assisting people with disabilities and economic disadvantages to start and operate their own small commercial ventures is another facet of social entrepreneurship that aligns well with social entrepreneurship theoretical frameworks. These frameworks aid in defining social entrepreneurship as "an innovative, social value creating activity that can occur within or across the nonprofit, business or government sectors" (Austin et al. 2006). Austin et al. posit a theoretical framework that aligns well with social entrepreneurship efforts to address income inequality among people with disabilities by assisting them to develop their own small commercial ventures, instead of providing wage-based jobs for groups of people.

The authors offer that social entrepreneurship is a dynamic fit between four interrelated concepts (the OCPD Framework): (1) "**O**pportunity" (a desired future state that is different than the current state and achievable), (2) "**C**ontext" (factors outside the control of management but that affect the venture), (3) "**P**eople and Resources" (the human and financial capital inputs supporting the venture), and (4) "**D**eals" (mutually beneficial arrangements between the venture and all resource providers). The OCPD social entrepreneurship theory correlates well with Inclusive Entrepreneurship and is relevant to situations like that presented in the case example in a number of ways.

Inclusive Entrepreneurship grew from a seed development grant provided by the U.S. Department of Labor/Office of Disability Employment Policy (ODEP) to test and demonstrate new self-employment methods for people with disabilities. The *Opportunity* in this case was not only the availability of a three-year government demonstration grant, but also the interest of ODEP policymakers to test how people with disabilities could increase their economic self-reliance as independent business owners rather than being relegated to either unemployment, full reliance on government social welfare benefits, or as workers in sheltered, segregated workshops. The high unemployment rate of people with disabilities in the United States and the relatively underutilized method of assisting them to become self-employed also created opportunities. The *Context* included a national movement promoting least restrictive, individualized and integrated work for people with disabilities, articulated in federal and state policies that self-employment naturally achieves. Also, the Syracuse University Institute that managed the project had longstanding knowledge and expertise in researching and applying practical knowledge in new venture creation for people with disabilities and was familiar with negotiating the policy, practice, and economic aspects of new venture creation. *People and Resources* were generated not only by the grant funding and by the Syracuse University team, but also by the project's commitment to develop cross-sector partnerships with business development agencies, disability services providers, government social service and economic departments, and others to mobilize their support of the effort. And the desire for people to become more independent and increase their income as entrepreneurs contributed to an enrollment in the project of over 225 people with disabilities and the creation of over 60 small business ventures. The *Deal* was evidenced by leveraging the grant resources, cross-sector partnerships, the academic environment that supported the creation of the Inclusive Entrepreneurship class (the source of the case example), and the dreams and talents of prospective entrepreneurs as well to establish their own commercial ventures. Consequently, promoting opportunities for people with disabilities and/or disadvantages as individual entrepreneurs as a form of social entrepreneurship correlates well with theoretical foundations supporting social entrepreneurship in general. As such, it lends itself to replication in other communities and countries seeking to address income inequality among the over 15 percent of the world's population that live with disabilities (World Health Organization 2014).

The Inclusive Entrepreneurship Template provides a structure for discussing and analyzing new venture start-ups (see Table 10.1). As students review the case example, they will identify as many of the factors shown

Table 10.1 Inclusive entrepreneurship template

Individual-Centric	Venture-Centric	Context-Centric
The Entrepreneur	*Operational Infrastructure*	*New Venture & Social Contexts*
Individual characteristics including age; motivation for starting the small venture; family circumstances that affect the venture; financial circumstances/commitments that affect the venture; maturity; networks—personal, family and venture-related that assist in developing the small venture; effects of disability on venture operations (strengths and challenges); support needs—personal, family, and new venture and how they are or will be met; future outlook—expectations of hours worked, financial expectations, venture growth expectations; perceptions of the opportunity	*Existence of a financial record keeping system* including breakeven point, cash flow; systems for receivables (timeliness and amount); systems for payables (timeliness and amount); ease of system use; financial controls; budgeting and financial planning system for collection and payment of VAT and other taxes; accuracy of records; costing structures	*New venture creation environment* including forces creating the opportunity; key success factors to capitalize upon opportunity; definition of the target market; barriers to entry; competitor shortcomings or strengths; size and growth potential of the market; fit between opportunity and concept; window of opportunity; customer loyalties to competitors and switching costs
Experiential characteristics including training skills and credentials related to the specific venture being developed; history/experience related to the particular venture; educational, training background related to the particular venture	*New venture operations* including existence or need for a new venture plan that includes a marketing strategy and financial plan; facilities; equipment, human resource systems, supply chain, internal controls; health and safety; delivery; handling complaints and returns; hours of operation; capacity versus demand; resource productivity; purchasing policies; customer service; inventory management and storage costs; outsourcing; value of inventory; quality control; theft/pilferage; performance benchmarking ratios; technology	*Social context* including advantages or barriers to market entry that are disability-related; barriers to access for training and technical assistance; acceptance/support of entrepreneurship by disability—serving agencies; stigma and misconceptions about disability affecting the establishment and operations of a new small venture

in the following that are apparent or that they may infer from reading the case. They will base their answers to the challenge questions on their interpretations of these factors, and their perceived effects on the new venture start-up. They will recommend three possible solutions to challenges that the entrepreneur may face that are individual, venture-related, or contextual.

References and Additional Resources

"Aimee Mullins and Her 12 Pairs of Legs" accessed at www.ted.com/talks/aimee_mullins_prosthetic_aesthetics

Austin, J., H. Stevenson, and J. Wei Skillern. 2006. "Social and Commercial Entrepreneurship: Same, Different, or Both?" *Entrepreneurship Theory and Practice* 30, no. 1, pp. 1–22.

Dees, G., J. Emerson, and P. Economy. 2001. *Enterprising Nonprofits: A Toolkit for Social Entrepreneurs.* New York: John Wiley.

Defourney, J., and M. Nyssens, eds. 2008. "Social Enterprise in Europe: Recent Trends and Developments." Working paper Series, No. 08/01, Liege, Belgium: EMS European Research Network.

Goffman, I. 1961. *Asylums.* New York, NY: Anchor Books.

Gottlieb, A., W.N. Myhill, and P. Blanck. 2010. "Employment of People with Disabilities." In *International Encyclopedia of Rehabilitation,* eds. J.H. Stone and M. Blouin, available online at http://cirrie.buffalo.edu/encyclopedia/en/article/123/

Griffin, C., and D. Hammis. 2008. *Making Self-Employment Work for People with Disabilities,* 1–20. Baltimore: Brookes Publishing Company.

Hoogendoorn, B., E. Pennings, and R. Thurik. 2010. What Do We Know About Social Entrepreneurship: An Analysis of the Empirical Research. Erasmus School of Economics. Erasmus University. Rotterdam, Netherlands.

Killeen, M., M. Adya, and G. Shaheen. 2010. *Inclusive Entrepreneurship-Final Project Report.* Syracuse, NY: Syracuse University.

Moss, T.W., J.C. Short, G.T. Payne, and G.T. Lumpkin. 2010. "Dual Identities in Social Ventures: An Exploratory Study." *Entrepreneurship Theory and Practice* 35, no. 4, pp. 805–30.

Shaheen, G. 2011. "Inclusive Entrepreneurship." In *Academic Entrepreneurship and Community Engagement-Scholarship in Action and the Syracuse Miracle,* ed. B. Kingma. Cheltenham, UK: Edward Elgar Publishing Ltd.

Shaheen, G., and M. Killeen. 2010. Primer on the Start-UP NY 4 Phase Entrepreneurship Model. New York. Cornell University and Syracuse University: Medicaid Infrastructure Grant Report.

Walls, R.T., D.L. Dowler, K. Cordingly, L.E. Orslene, and J.D. Greer. 2001. "Microenterprising and People with Disabilities: Strategies for Success and Failure." *The Journal of Rehabilitation* 67, no. 2, pp. 29–35.

Warner, R., and J. Mandiberg. 2006. "An Update on Affirmative Businesses or Social Firms for People with Mental Illness." *Psychiatric Services* 57, no. 10, pp. 1488–92.

Wendell, S. 1996. "The Social Construction of Disability." Chapter 2, In *The Rejected Body: Feminist Philosophical Reflections on Disability.* New York, NY: Routledge.

Yunis, M. 2007. *Creating a World Without Poverty.* New York, NY: Public Affairs Publishing Company.

CHAPTER 11

Worksheet for "Contexts for Social Entrepreneurs"

Paul Miesing

University at Albany, State University of New York

Mission

What are its key philosophical values and core purpose (strategic intent)? What is your company's unique overall purpose? Does it:

> Articulate its reason for existence? *Explain:* _____
> _____
> Arouse a strong sense of socioeconomic or business purpose? *Explain:* _____
> Challenges and motivations? *Explain:* _____
> _____
> Bring your workforce together and galvanize your people to live the business? *Explain:* ___
> _____
> Meet the community's needs or other social needs? *Explain:* _____
> _____

Criterion	Comment
Concise (30 to 60 words) and *precise* (clear and simple) statement of core values and purpose	
Unique and *understandable* (states who you are … what you stand for)	
Cornerstone (short but everlasting foundation … that remains relevant)	
Flair (suitable for framing … and as a laminated card)	
Enthusiastic, *sincere*, *memorable*, and *motivational* (everyone willingly sings its hymns)	

Vision

How do you see your venture's role in society and the impact it will make? Does it:

Achieve desired accomplishments for long-term success? *Explain:* _____

Create a shared, aspired future state determined by full participation? *Explain:* _____

Identify competitive advantage of your goals? *Explain:* _____

Focus on stakeholders (external) rather than product and process (internal)? *Explain:* ____

Values

What is your company's culture and core purpose? Does it:

Have a unique cultural setting? *Explain:* _____

Share norms and values? *Explain:* _____

Encourage creating value for stakeholders? *Explain:* _____

Allow your organization to be fast and flexible to enter new markets, products, technologies, processes, and arrangements? *Explain:* _____

Allow your organization to create a sense of anxiety and urgency? *Explain:* _____

Seek consistency and integration for social goals? *Explain:* _____

Scope

Broadly define the scope of the venture's operations in product market terms. Does it include:

Target customers: Who is being served? *Explain:* _____

Value proposition: What needs are satisfied? *Explain:* _____

Social value: Does your organization create social value by being resourceful (e.g., improvise with limited resources or repurpose materials that appear to be useless)? _____
Supply chain: How create and deliver? *Explain:* _____

Stakeholders

For your organization, who will provide resources and what will they expect/demand?

Stakeholder	Resources	Expectations
Funder(s)		
Clients		
Personnel		
Community		
Government(s)		
Partners and Allies		
Other		
Other		

PART III

Recognizing, Pitching, and Communicating Social Opportunities

CHAPTER 12

Best Social Enterprise Pitch Competition

Jerrid P. Kalakay

Valencia College

Introduction

This exercise enhances the overall understanding of social enterprise planning, operations, and the value it can have in the market place. This exercise furthers the development of students' social entrepreneurial skill-set, increased self-confidence, risk-taking propensity.

Purpose/Learning Objectives

The social enterprise pitch competition has roots in business plan competitions, which, first appeared in the early 1980s at the University of Texas (Bell 2010). The traditional business plan competitions have evolved into pitch competitions as the nature of entrepreneurship has evolved. The pitch competition helps to promote social entrepreneurship by providing an avenue to students with ideas and those involved with start-ups (e.g., business angels, venture capitalists, serial entrepreneurs) to network, discover, develop, and exploit plentiful business ideas (Foo, Wong, and Ong 2005; Huffman and Quigley 2002). This is an experiential exercise that will require students to develop an effective and articulate message of the current and prospective value their social enterprise provides or will provide. This process also allows students to move their messaging from a generic social good language toward a specific value-added language that more adequately addresses specific audience needs.

Wadhwa (2010) concluded, from his reflections on entrepreneurial education, the key is to provide education at teachable moments—when the entrepreneur is thinking about starting a venture or ready to scale it. What entrepreneurs need is not the type of abstract course they teach at business schools, but practical, relevant knowledge. There is a real need to allow social entrepreneurial students opportunities to gain practical relevant knowledge and experience. The real prize in the social enterprise pitch competition is the opportunity it provides for students to further develop their ideas and enterprises.

Time Required

Conducting this exercise will likely take an entire class session. While not required, a computer with a projector is necessary if the competition will include the use of multimedia (check with your instructor).

Exercise Schedule

The exercise has six major components: (1) initial brainstorming session on current or potential social enterprises to pitch; (2) crafting a professional pitch; (3) presenting your pitch to your instructor, classmates, and potential guests; (4) answering pitch-related questions from instructor, classmates, and potential guests; (5) gaining feedback from instructor, classmates, and potential guests; (6) conducting a debriefing and reflection session on your pitch and corresponding feedback.

Assignment

There are five steps to this exercise.

1. Pre-reading and preparation work
   For this exercise, you will be expected to read the assigned articles and complete the major components (1) and (2) in the aforementioned exercise schedule.
   S. Gerber, *6 Steps to the Perfect Pitch* available at www.entrepreneur. com/article/201826

K.D. Elsbach, *How to Pitch a Brilliant Idea* available at https://hbr.org/2003/09/how-to-pitch-a-brilliant-idea

S. Waldron, *Master Your Nerves: Four Steps to Delivering a Great Business Pitch* available at www.theguardian.com/small-business-network/2015/jul/07/master-nerves-four-steps-delivering-great-business-pitch

When crafting your pitch, be sure to include the answers to the following questions. The following questions should be addressed in your 2- to 5-minute pitch.

1. What problem are you trying to solve?
2. What is your proposed innovative enterprise? Why is it important? How will you launch or scale the enterprise?
3. What evidence do you have that this enterprise will solve the stated problem? What measurements will you use to evaluate your enterprise?
4. Who is/will be leading this enterprise and what are their qualifications? What are the current or proposed funding sources or revenues?
5. What are your current enterprise needs? What is your "Ask"?
6. Any additional questions your instructor would like you to include.

2. Presenting your pitch

You will have between 2 and 5 minutes in total for your pitch (please ask your instructor for the exact length in time). The pitch begins with a brief explanation of the competition and rules.

1. At minimum one member of each team must be an enrolled student in the course.
2. Each team must also have no less than two members and no more than five members.
3. The proposed enterprise should not be in violation of any intellectual property rights or unlawful in any manner.
4. Each team should strictly follow the time limit for their pitch.

Your pitch will be followed by a 10-minute question and answer session with your instructor, classmates, and potential guests.

3. Gain feedback

After your pitch and Q & A session, your instructor, classmates, and potential guests will provide you a 5-minute feedback session on your pitch. This feedback will be on your overall delivery, the enterprise idea, clarity, potential value, the probability of success, along with other potential points of feedback.

4. Debrief and reflection

The true value of this exercise comes from the knowledge and experience gained from pitching your enterprise. This is only realized upon a careful debrief and reflection session with your team. This debrief should be taken seriously and your team should openly discuss the questions asked and the feedback given. The questions and feedback that your team received were designed to assist your team in improving your pitch. Your team should make the necessary revisions to your pitch needed.

5. Personal reflection on pitch

Lastly, this exercise requires each student to write a one-page personal reflection on this experience participating in the social enterprise pitch competition. This reflection should answer the following questions: What have I learned from participating in this social enterprise pitch competition? What about my pitch would I change if I were to participate in a future competition?

References and Additional Resources

Bell, J. 2010. "Student Business Plan Competitions: Who Really Does have Access?" In *Small Business Institute*® National Proceedings: 18.

Bliemel, M.J. 2014. "Getting Entrepreneurship Education out of the Classroom and into Students' Heads." *Entrepreneurship Research Journal* 4, no. 2, pp. 237–60.

Foo, M.D., P.K. Wong, and A. Ong. 2005. "Two Others Think You Have a Viable Business Idea? Team Diversity and Judges a Valuation of Ideas in Business Plan Competition." *Journal of Business Venturing* 20, no. 3, pp. 385–402.

Wadhwa, V. 2010. "Can Entrepreneurs Be Made?" *TechCrunch* http://techcrunch.com/2010/02/27/can-entrepreneurs-be-made/ (accessed February 27).

CHAPTER 13

Mapping Stakeholders and Developing Communication Strategies

Rachida Justo

IE Business School/IE University

Rakhi Mehra

MHS City Lab

Ashley King-Bischof

Mavuno

Introduction

Increasing calls for organizations to demonstrate "corporate citizenship" have raised an entrepreneur's awareness of the need to be accountable to a broad range of stakeholders beyond investors and customers (Preston and Sapienza 1990) and, as such, make them part of the communication loop (Cornelissen 2014). While this has given rise to several academic studies on communication strategy and management for companies, these subjects are still notoriously absent from social entrepreneurship research (Dorigo and Marcon 2014). This is surprising given the major role that multiple stakeholders, institutions, and networks play in the success and growth of social enterprises (Defourny and Nyssens 2006; Di Domenico, Haugh, and Tracey 2010).

Social entrepreneurs (SE) and their ventures are indeed part of a larger ecosystem with multiple agencies and actors. Due to the magnitude and complexity of social problems, which span across sectors and institutional boundaries, SE need to account for the needs of a diverse set of actors who have a "stake" or interest in the social problem being tackled (Dorado 2006). The financial and nonfinancial stakeholders to which an SE are readily accountable to, are generally greater in number and more varied than those of traditional entrepreneurs, resulting in greater complexity in managing these relationships (Kanter and Summers 1987). SE also needs to pursue alliance and communication approaches as a means to mobilizing resources, financial and nonfinancial, from the larger context to achieve increased impact.

Beyond pure academic research, issues related to stakeholder analysis and communication strategy are also largely lacking from educational curricula on social entrepreneurship (see for example Howorth et al. 2012; Litzky et al. 2009; Miller et al. 2012). As a result, SE often start by identifying and prioritizing the end users and funding organizations, but lack a clear engagement strategy with other stakeholders that can directly or indirectly influence the project outcomes. Moreover, while budding SE are generally trained to pitch their projects to potential investors, they often neglect the boarder audience of stakeholders that is specifically relevant for social enterprises. These include donors, national or political actors (e.g., legislators, governors), interest groups (e.g., unions, associations), commercial/private for-profit, nonprofit organizations, and civil society members.

The present exercise is aimed at addressing these gaps by introducing frameworks for identifying stakeholders, mapping and including them in the social venture's communication strategy—to be tailored accordingly to the audience with consistent messaging. The paper is envisaged in four sections. The first section will briefly review academic literature on the topic. The second section will introduce how SE should approach mapping their stakeholders. Third, and with the stakeholder map made, we will focus on designing tailored communication approaches. In the last sections, two real cases of social ventures will be used as an illustrative hands-on exercise that could be used in the classroom for social entrepreneurship students.

Purpose/Learning Objectives

The specific learning objectives include the following:

- Identify and map key stakeholders.
- Understand the sources of value that might drive a fruitful partnership with key stakeholders.
- Develop communication skills that are tailored to the needs of SE and the diverse range of stakeholders they need to ally to their cause.

Time Required

This exercise can be implemented in one or two class sessions of 80 minutes each (plus prework). The length will depend on the number of student groups and the number of cases used as an illustration.

Exercise Schedule

The following schedule is designed for a one-session exercise format:

- Step 1: 10 minutes
- Step 2: 25 minutes
- Step 3: 15 minutes
- Step 4: 15 minutes
- Step 5: 25 minutes

1. Prework

   Although this is not necessary, to save time for class discussion and encourage students to think in advance about the topic, the instructor can distribute Template I on "Identifying and Analyzing Stakeholders" in the session before the exercise. In that case, students will be required to come to class after having filled in the template (individually or in groups) with the information related to the social venture they are working on.

2. Conduct group discussion and work on identifying and mapping stakeholders

   The exercise will start with an analytical discussion on the use of stakeholder analysis and mapping. In his classic book, Freeman

(1984) defined a stakeholder as "…any group or individual who can affect or is affected by the achievement of the organization's purpose and objectives." Stakeholders are therefore organizations/individuals who have interest and/or influence in a SE's problem, organization, personnel, project, solution, or customers. Although organization called "Sam" originated from business sciences, it now incorporates political and environmental sciences and has been widely adopted in the nonprofit sector and by multilateral agencies.

Background on Identifying Stakeholders

The first step students should go through is identifying the potential stakeholders of the social venture they are working on. In his stakeholder model of the organization, Cornelissen (2014) suggests that the different stakeholders of the organization need to be identified and must be addressed for the stake that they hold. Addressing stakeholder means providing them with the type of information about the organization's activities that they have an interest in. Donors and impact investors, for example, will need to be provided with financial and social performance information (e.g., through impact metrics included in periodic reports), while customers and beneficiaries need to be supplied with information about products and services. Following is a nonexhaustive list of the range of actors that SE should consider including in their list of stakeholders. The instructor should help students systematically go through each of these categories and draw a through a list of potential actors/organizations within each category for their organizations.

Customers and/or Target Beneficiaries

The principal recipient of the value created by social businesses is, in most cases, poor and marginalized populations (Alvord et al. 2004). Literature suggests that the real success of SE lies not only in creating information and resources that are available and user-friendly for the local (marginalized) population (Alvord et al. 2004; Zahra et al. 2009) but also in establishing an appropriate communication strategy with the principal recipient of the social venture (Russel 2004). A recent research undertaken by Acumen Fund and Bain & Company suggests for example that in order to spur greater adoption of agricultural innovations, SE had to systematically ensure that the "Four As" (awareness, advantage, affordability, and access) were continuously in place for their farmer customers. Two of these elements deal with communication. Specifically, *Adoption* starts with an unrelenting focus on the farmer: how to raise his or her awareness of new products and services. *Advantage*, in turn, refers to how to communicate and reliably deliver on the advantage the farmer will gain by adopting innovations (Bain & Company Inc. 2014).

Donors/Impact Investors and Other Resource Providers

In order to access funds, the SE must know how to attract the interest of donors, investors, and/or institutional fund providers. At the start-up phase, some scholars argue that governments, NGOs, and charitable foundations are the usual sources of funding for SE (Zahra et al. 2009). At later stages, Dacin et al. (2010) argue that SE tend to collaborate among each other, using resources in a cooperative fashion, and often actually share these with other organizations. The scope of the social needs to be addressed also usually requires establishing strategic collaborations with for-profit corporations, thereby further increasing the diversity of the stakeholders. For example, Zahra et al. (2009) identify the need of SE to know how to communicate with decently large and complex organization.

Employees and Volunteers

SE, with their limited capacity for offering financial incentives, often pay below-market rates and rely heavily on volunteer labor. Consequently, they must often rely less on financial rewards and incentives and more on intrinsic motivators and creative strategies for attracting, motivating, and retaining staff (Wei-Skillern et al. 2007). This makes the role of the founder(s) as inspirational leader(s) fundamental. In particular, an appropriate communication strategy is key to gain employee's emotional buy-in to the mission (Ilies et al. 2006) and encourage them to achieve higher performance standards despite relatively low financial incentives.

Community, NGOs, and the Broader Environment

One of the greatest skills of any SE is their ability to inspire, marshal, and mobilize the efforts of the community and their broader environment in the pursuit of social wealth. Zahra et al. (2009) argue that for social engineers harnessing popular support is the only escape to the lack of legitimacy they may face when focusing on their mission.

Background on Mapping Stakeholders

Once a list of stakeholders is established, the instructor should ask students to start analyzing the organization's stakeholders and their influence and interest in the social venture. Scholars propose several forms of stakeholder analysis that the instructor can choose from. For this exercise, we have chosen a set of basic questions provided by Carroll (1989). These help capture the essential information needed for effective stakeholder communication:

1. Who are the organization's stakeholders?
2. What are their stakes?
3. What opportunities and challenges are presented to the organization in relation to these stakeholders, and possible social goals?
4. What responsibilities (social, economic, legal, etc.) does the organization have to all its stakeholders?
5. In what way can the organization best communicate with and respond to these stakeholders and address these stakeholder challenges and opportunities in relation to social responsibilities?

A similar approach is to use a mapping or model to identify and position stakeholders in terms of their influence on the organization's operations or in terms of their stance on a particular social issue or target beneficiary that the social enterprise intends to address. A mapping device that communication practitioners often use in the management field is the power-interest matrix (e.g., Ackerman and Eden 2011; Cornelissen 2011). In this exercise, we will rely on a similar mapping tool that is commonly used by multinational organizations like the World Bank: the *influence-interest matrix* (Fritz, Levy, and Ort 2014). Both tools are meant to enhance the SE's knowledge of stakeholders and their influence, and enable her to plan an appropriate communication strategy, both at the start-up phase, as well as on an ongoing basis.

While some instructors might choose to distribute information to the students on this matrix prior to class, we rather recommend fostering a class discussion on the subject. Ideally, students should come up to the conclusion that one of the most effective ways to categorize stakeholders is by looking at (a) the power or influence that they possess, and (b) the extent to which they are likely to have or show an interest in the social enterprise's activities. We define *influence* as the ability of a particular stakeholder to change the process, people, or outcomes in the SE's project. Interest, in turn, refers to stakeholders a demonstrated or potential awareness about and concern for the SE's activities or impact. Each stakeholder will have high or low influence on and a high or low interest in the SE's project and outcomes.

When mapping stakeholders, students should:

1. Use a grid/matrix with axis of influence and interest from low to high.
2. Plot each stakeholder in the appropriate spot inside the matrix.

Because of the gradation in the SE's matrix, stakeholders should be ranked in order and grouped into quadrants. Each quadrant in a map has a set of stakeholders that can be labeled as such with social goals:

1. Promoters (high interest in the social aspect, high influence)
2. Defenders (high interest, low influence)
3. Latents (low interest, high influence)
4. Apathetics (low interest, low influence)

3. Conduct class discussion on designing a communication strategy
   Once the students have a prepared list of stakeholders and know their interest and influence in their project, they should prepare for each, a plan to communicate their project with promotion of social aspects of the project.

Engaging Promoters

Promoters are the stakeholders with the most influence and interest; they will be the most important stakeholders to a social venture and should be attended to accordingly. Students will quickly conclude that most of an SE's engagement strategy will focus on them, even though they are not the only part of it. The instructor should facilitate a discussion on the steps that need to be taken in order to actively engage these stakeholders. Insights such as the following can emerge from the discussion:

1. Identify the one individual who is the representation of the stakeholder (e.g., VP of Marketing at NGO).
2. Get the contact details of those individuals.
3. Set up an early conversation with them to understand more about their influence and interest in your project. Use this opportunity to give them an early view of your proposed project, but offer promoters an opportunity to exercise their influence on the project first.
4. Iterate on your project. Use the feedback from stakeholders to make any changes that could benefit you both.
5. Set up a second conversation to address their interest, and leverage their influence to promote your project.

Informing Defenders

These are the social enterprise big supporters, but unfortunately they have little say in the current success of the organization. Some students might argue that they need to provide defenders with information about the project with a social aim and that involving them continues their support. Indeed, not engaging them may turn them away, and could hurt your project if they gain more influence. Still, the instructor should make students realize that their communication strategy with them should be as efficient as possible as they will seek a lot of their time. For example, using e-mail or social media channels could help keep them informed without requiring personal one-on-one time with each of them.

Advocating to Latents

These stakeholders may not have interest to collaborate or formally engage with the project or not see value in the project's offering. However, latents have considerable influence over project outcome and other key stakeholders and thus a strategy to affiliate with them or enhance their interest is important. Communicating with this stakeholder may require consistent advocacy strategy, behavioral change efforts, identifying early adopters and/or outreach efforts at multiple levels through identification with other organizations or platforms of interest to the stakeholder.

Informing Apathetics

Those are stakeholders with the least influence and least interest. Apathetics may not even know that the SE's project or organization exists, so students will generally quickly agree that they should be given much less consideration. This category of stakeholders will therefore be given the least time and attention in this exercise. The instructor may however mention that SE's need to keep track of them in case they move to another quadrant.

4. Students' pitches

   Time permitting, students should get back to work in groups and try to prepare a pitch to members from another team for a more interactive and live discussion. Depending on time availability and whether this is a one session or two session course, for this last part of the session the professor can randomly select one, two, or several groups to pitch in front of the class (or ask for volunteers). The instructor can facilitate the following questions to help students prepare the pitch:

   1. What is the need of this stakeholder?
   2. Does your project fulfill their need? If so, how does your project fill their need?
   3. Does your project impede on this stakeholder? If so, how? If so, how can you mitigate or offer something better for them?
   4. How does the partnership look? What are the details of your potential arrangement?
   5. What are you asking from them?
   6. What are the details of the timeline?

After the presentation, the instructor can emphasize the key points that emerged from the pitches, and the potential questions that remained unsolved. S/he could then distribute Template III for students to take home.

5. Postwork

While the exercise does not include any specific postwork, students should be encouraged to apply the frameworks discussed in class to the social projects they are working on.

Templates

Template I: Identifying and Analyzing Stakeholders

Stakeholder	Organization/ Department/ Individual or Group	Internal/ External	Level of interest	Level of influence
Government/Regulatory agencies				
Customers/ Target beneficiaries				
Employees/ Cofounders				
Industry				
Community				
Media				
Civil society orgs				
Investors/Funders				
Research agencies, universities				

Template II: Mapping Stakeholders—Interest/Influence Matrix

DEFENDERS	PROMOTERS
APATHETICS	LATENTS

Template III: The Communication Toolkit

1	*The need*	The unanswered stakeholder need that agency can help solve
2	*How agency fills it*	The assets agency brings to the relationship in order to address the stakeholder's need
3	*Key benefits*	What benefits will this partnership offer generally?
4	*WIIFM*	How will the stakeholder personally benefit from this partnership? What's in it for me!
5	*How to Partner*	The strengths that agency will leverage in order to work or partner with the stakeholder
6	*The ask*	What you are asking from the stakeholder?

Illustrative Cases for Class Discussion

In order to reinforce student's learning and comprehension of the concepts and frameworks introduced in this exercise, it is recommended that the instructor uses (one of) the two cases presented in the following, as practical examples in each of the steps described previously. This might be especially helpful if the exercise is administered to undergraduate students or students who do not have a business and/or social sector background. Alternatively, the instructor might choose to distribute the examples to students as a postwork reading.

1. Case study 1: mHS City Lab

mHS's Mission and Project

Founded in 2009, mHS is an interdisciplinary social enterprise launched to foster socially inclusive cities and design innovative solutions for low-income housing. As an action research agency, it has adopted a two-pronged strategy: (a) incubate innovative projects for proof of concept, and (b) undertake research to influence and inform policies on urban development and disseminate field insights. This strategy requires engaging across a broad range of stakeholders at a strategic, operational, funding, and collaborative level.

The goal of mHS's core project on self-construction/incremental housing is to improve quality of housing in informal settlements. Informal settlements or "slums" are to be considered part of the solution to the housing crisis. Despite all the shortcomings, incremental home construction in a bottom-up process that is needs-based and taps local skills, networks, and resources. While there are certain slum locations that are unfit for human habitation, majority are bustling centers of social and economic activity providing affordable rentals and shelter to a large section of the city's population. mHS's thesis is that the construction process needs to be appropriately facilitated and improved not stifled and demolished. The project initiatives include (a) deliver access to technical know-how for unengineered structures, (b) improve quality of skills of construction labor (c) access to finance for construction and home improvements, and (d) a more inclusive policy environment for self-built incremental housing neighborhoods.

Mapping and Prioritizing mHS Project Stakeholders

Stakeholder	mHS	Nature	Interest	Influence
Government/ Regulatory agencies	Municipality Urban Development Ministry Housing Ministry Multilateral agencies/ National Housing Bank National Disaster Management Authority (NDMA)	External	Low	High
Customers/ Target beneficiaries	Masons, Contractors Home Owners	External	Low/Med	High
Employees/ Cofounders	Architects, Engineers Social, Anthropologists Inclusive Finance	Internal	High Med High	High Med High
Industry/Private sector	Microfinance Institutions, Real Estate, Construction Materials	External	Med	Medium to high
Community	Resident Welfare Associations, Political Candidates	External	Low Low	Low High
Media	National International Platforms	Internal	Med High	Med Med

(Continued)

Stakeholder	mHS	Nature	Interest	Influence
Civil society orgs	Skill Development Housing Rights Slum Upgradation Water and Sanitation	External	Med	High
Investors/Funders	National Multilateral	Internal/ External	Low High	Med Low
Research agencies, universities	Architectures, Engineering, Urban Development	External	Med	Med

Ranking mHS Stakeholders' Influence and Interest

DEFENDERS Media Research/Academic Departments Civil Society Organizations	**PROMOTERS** Employees/ Cofounders Microfinance Institutions
APATHETICS Resident Welfare Associations Political Representatives	**LATENTS** Government Agencies Masons Home Owners Cement Companies

Communicating with Stakeholders

In what follows is a list of the main stakeholders in each quadrant as well as a short pitch following the communication toolkit outlined in Section 4.5.

Promoters

- BASIX—a national Microfinance Institution (MFI)
- World Bank
- Michael and Susan Dell Foundation (MSDF)

Understanding first which agency/organization to partner with required some networking and understanding for fit on culture, process, and a trust-based relationship that would allow for experimentation. mHS met with several MFIs for partnership and identified BASIX through previous interactions as the best fit for the pilot. It was however unclear at first if the pilot should be housed with the R&D team or as part of the mainstream credit activities, and thus we pitched to different teams at BASIX, an interactive process that lasted close to 4 months. Our previous work experience with MFIs gave inroads to researching end customer needs and analyzes how they were deploying the loans. Communicating with BASIX—what we learnt about their customers and their aspirations on housing—was critical to entice their interest levels. Identifying the funding partner, MSDF has recently begun to fund housing ventures and known to support early-stage experimentations. They were looking for credibility and partnerships already in place. The World Bank collaboration came after the pilot phase was completed and the insights was an opportunity to influence design of a large-scale US$ 100 million refinance facility where mHS was engaged as consultants.

Pitch to Microfinance Agencies (National Head of Innovation)

- Your customers are deploying over 25 percent of personal or livelihood loans for home improvement purposes (1). A specialized housing product would better suit the repayment terms, monitor end use, and allow customers to construction know-how at affordable rates (3). Once a house customer show loyalty, you may be able to cross-selling and you may expand the frontiers of financial inclusion (4). Launching a pilot over 18 months, where mHS brings technical expertise and BASIX brings the financial product innovation would provide the necessary environment (5).

Pitch to the Michael and Susan Dell Foundation

- mHS is collaborating with BASIX to launch a pilot that brings housing microfinance and quality construction know-how to microfinance clientele. Over 70 percent of housing is self-built; however it relies on prohibitively expensive informal finance with low-income households living in precarious structures. We would value MSDF's financial and knowledge support (5) to embark on an action research project that has potential to scale across other financial institutions and influence government policy on incremental housing.

Pitch to the World Bank Private Sector Team

- We understand that the Bank is collaborating with the Government of India/National Housing Bank on a Low Income Housing Finance Project. As the project is in the design phase (1) we can add value and provide key insights from a pilot conducted on lending in informal areas (2). The most important takeaway was the opportunity to impact construction quality, and willingness of homeowners to pay for technical advice (3).

Defenders

- The Centre for Policy Research (CPR) had been a defender in the early stages of the project—we had sought their advice and consulted them at several steps, included hosting CPR interns and being available for research-related questions. We also attended events on urbanization hosted by them. When we wanted to organize a national level discussion on the issue of informal settlements and housing, CPR would be an ideal partner to gather the representatives and bring the issue to the frontline.

Pitch to the Centre for Policy Research

- mHS's experience is incremental housing in urban informal settlements (2) and we believe it is timely to influence the Government's approach to slum upgradation (1). We wanted to discuss a potential collaboration (5) with CPR to co-organize a national level workshop on informality, providing a forum to engage government representatives (3). This would complement CPR's research interest on urbanization trends and provide insights into governance level challenges (4).

Apathetic

- Resident Welfare Associations
- Political Representatives
- Cement Companies

Despite sale to the informal construction segment, cement companies do not have a direct engagement strategy to influence the quality of construction. As formal building plan approvals are not required/feasible, architects and engineers are not involved in the design, construction, and monitoring process. Cement companies could have greater involvement in how cement is to be mixed, advising on multistory construction with reinforced cement concrete (RCC) to ensure structural integrity. However, interest levels are low in the current climate and policy environment on informal housing. In the future, cement companies could have greater influence and be involved in training of construction manpower, and introducing new materials better suited for self-construction. Our engagement strategy would be to engage with Industry Associations (instead of companies), generate interest through change in policy, CSR involvement, and newsletter updates.

Latents

- Masons and Contractors
- Municipality of Delhi

All municipalities have the mandate to improve slum conditions and provide basic services to low-income households. The aim was to position self-construction as a low hanging fruit, as compared with rehabilitation and rebuilding projects that are time and resource intensive. We wanted to communicate that upgrading slums had multiple benefits: a lower subsidy requirement, building on an existing knowledge base, and leveraging resources of civil society organizations. The challenge was concerning legality and security of tenure, which determined the ability of households to access formal finance. Engagement strategy was to increase interest level and "be heard" through collaborating with recognized civil society agencies and gathering media coverage.

Masons

Engagement Strategy: It was critical to get the masons excited about upgrading their skills on construction practices and bring greater awareness on disaster-safe construction. These target groups have previously not received formal training and have no access to technical know-how. The one strategy to enhance their interest level was to "learn by doing" during a pilot and provide an opportunity to "experience" the benefit of a knowledge exchange without undermining their experience. Word of mouth would be the most effective channel to begin with. Other incentives/benefits are to highlight the possibility for enhancing income and gaining certification for vocational skills.

2. Case study 2: Mavuno

Mavuno Background, Current Phase and Needs

Founded by MBA students at IE Business School (Madrid, Spain) in 2014, Mavuno is a social enterprise with a mission to improve the incomes of famers by supplying technologies that enhance the production and distribution in agricultural sectors.

Mavuno has developed an SMS-based platform that allows farmers to auction their harvests to wholesale buyers through their mobile phones. Mavuno currently has one full-time cofounder and a part-time software developer, with a small team of advisors. With a working prototype, the next phase of Mavuno is to launch a pilot in Western Kenya to test its first product. Mavuno will be seeking partnerships for this pilot phase, to include seed funders, a distribution method, 100 to 500 farmers, and two field staff. In order to launch the pilot program, Mavuno needs to appropriately understand who the key stakeholders are at this stage in the enterprise, and engage each in a way that is the most efficient and effective.

Mapping and Prioritizing Mavuno's Project Stakeholders

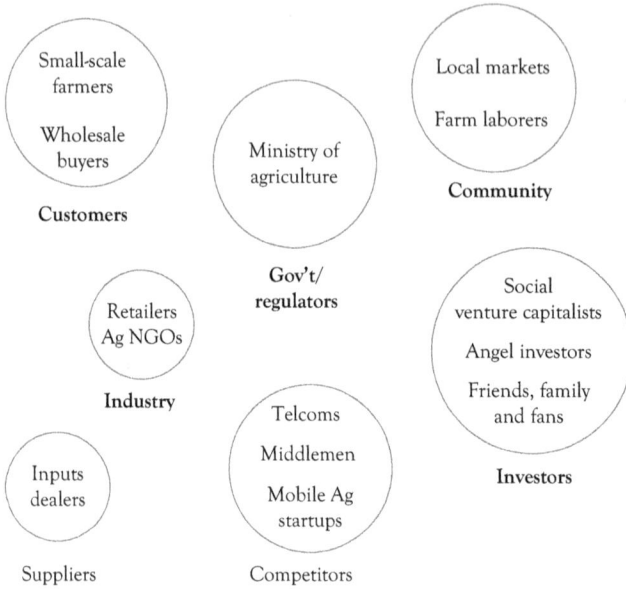

Small-scale farmers

Wholesale buyers

Customers

Ministry of agriculture

Gov't/ regulators

Local markets

Farm laborers

Community

Retailers
Ag NGOs

Industry

Social venture capitalists

Angel investors

Friends, family and fans

Investors

Inputs dealers

Suppliers

Telcoms

Middlemen

Mobile Ag startups

Competitors

Ranking Stakeholders' Influence and Interest

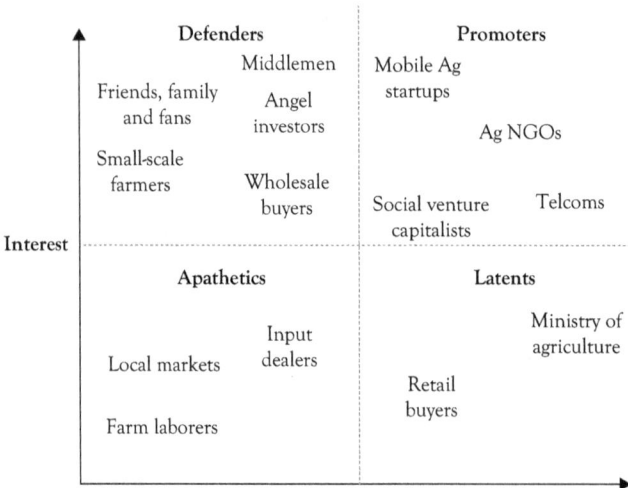

	Defenders	Promoters
	Middlemen	Mobile Ag startups
	Friends, family and fans	Angel investors	Ag NGOs
	Small-scale farmers	Wholesale buyers	
Interest		Social venture capitalists Telcoms
	Apathetics	Latents
		Input dealers	Ministry of agriculture
	Local markets	Retail buyers
	Farm laborers	

Communicating with Stakeholders

Promoters

- Agricultural Nongovernmental Organizations
- Social Venture Capitalists
- Telecoms

Each of the Promoters needs a very specific conversation with a key decision maker within the organization. When Mavuno meets with them, it will be important to have a very thorough pitch ready that addresses their needs and attracts them to the pilot project. Here are a few examples:

Pitch to the Agricultural Nongovernmental Organization—Western Kenya—Managing Director

> As your mission is to empower the chronically hungry to pull themselves out of poverty, you know that not only crop production but perhaps more important is market access for farmers to sell their crops into a larger market with high demand. Mavuno has a perfectly aligned mission. Our goal is to increase farmer incomes by making their markets more efficient. We are piloting a platform that is unique to the Kenyan market, but proven popular in Uganda by a Google-funded research team. We believe that your farmers could benefit from an easy-to-use digital platform in order to increase their incomes. In alignment with OAF's operations, we propose a joint trial of our product from January to December, two seasons. Mavuno will implement the technology with 1,000 farmers and OAF will allow us to use its communication channels and a few hours a month of 10 field officers time in co-branding our product.

Pitch to the Social Venture Capitalist—Africa-Based Fund—Managing Director

> You are working within agricultural transformation, technology leapfrogging and the mobile revolution. With our product, we can do all three. We are setting up partnerships that allow us to understand the local rules and have deep roots. Our management team is made up of individuals with backgrounds that prove they can execute entrepreneurial endeavors and manage large projects. With this combination, we could add great value to your portfolio. We are completing the first half of our pilot project in 2015 and will look for seed funding come June. We are asking for $100,000 for a 15 percent equity stake. We would first like to talk about exit options, as we know that's important to your firm.

Pitch to Telecom—Safaricom—Member of Innovation Board

> Safaricom has a unique position in the Kenyan market, but due
> to price wars with competitors it's apparent that you need to con-
> tinue to innovate and produce new applications to increase user-
> ship or have additional non-voice channels of revenue. Partnering
> with Mavuno will give you both. Our partnerships benefit us not
> only in using MPesa but also that Safaricom's the most admired
> brand. We can push that further by reaching a cash-based econ-
> omy of farmers in rural regions of Kenya. 64 percent of our cus-
> tomers said they were willing to trade their crops via SMS. That's
> a huge market potential for you. We are beginning a pilot of our
> prototype and we would like to partner with you from the begin-
> ning. Access to technical knowledge on your technology. We hold
> the IP but give you first right of refusal in contracts in Kenya. You
> take home your 40 percent of profits. Equity stake is negotiable.
> Let's start this in July 2015.

Defenders

- Friends, Family and Fans
- Middlemen
- Angel Investors
- Wholesale Buyers

Defenders in the context of Mavuno's pilot will want to keep abreast
of the activities, milestones, and accomplishments. As they have less
influence than Promoters, they should require less individual attention.
However, Mavuno will want to address their need of feeling connected
(as to keep their interest levels high). This is important, as they may, in
either this phase of Mavuno or another, gain more influence for Mavuno.

In order to fulfill their need, Mavuno should write a monthly newsletter to those who have shown particular interest in the beginning stages
of Mavuno. The newsletter will be mass e-mailed and only needs to be
drafted once. This newsletter can remain exclusive and advertised as
such. They can receive full details on how their contribution has made
an impact on the pilot project: perhaps they invested in the pilot, or they

provided resources that made it successful. It may be effective to include a story or two from the field as most of them will not reside in Kenya.

Latents

- Ministry of Agriculture
- Retail Buyers

The Ministry of Agriculture in Kenya and retail buyers are too large of a group to be concerned with a small, short-term pilot. Our engagement strategy should anticipate that there might be a word-of-mouth communication channel that gets information to these stakeholders during the pilot. Internally, Mavuno should have a 30-second description of their mission, the purpose of the current activities, and the potential for social impact. Mavuno will want to tailor the message so that these stakeholders do not get involved before we are ready to engage them like Promoters.

30-Second Pitch:

Mavuno is a social enterprise with a mission to improve the incomes of famers by supplying technologies that enhance the production and distribution in agricultural sectors. Mavuno is doing research on the needs of small-scale farmers in Kenya to understand how it can address them with technological solutions. The pilot project is a very small project intended to work solely with farmers as they harvest and sell their products in their local markets.

Apathetics

- Local markets
- Input dealers
- Farm laborers

While apathetics are very large groups of individuals, they are weakly connected cross Kenya. During the pilot phase, Mavuno will not engage them, unless we come across them. Given that this is a social enterprise that aims to increase income on farms, when that happens, some of the apathetics may increase in interest, especially if they believe they are not receiving some of that income.

Action item: During the pilot, understand the influence that the apathetics have on farm owners and vice versa, so that in the future we can anticipate communication channels and timing for engagement when they move from apathetics to defenders.

Monitoring Mavuno's Stakeholders

After one month of the pilot, Mavuno will reevaluate the impact that its project has had on the interest of its stakeholders, and review the level of influence of the most critical stakeholders. Particularly, because one of Mavuno's main competitors is known to have a high burn rate and is still seeking investment, they could quickly run out of money and lose the high level of influence they currently have. This would relieve Mavuno of a lot of work managing the competitor and their strategies.

Additionally, if the pilot goes well, or significantly disrupts normal distribution of goods, middlemen may reach out to government officials of the Ministry of Agriculture and create a change in the interest of this stakeholder. If this occurs, it would move the Ministry of Agriculture into the Promoter region of the Stakeholder Quadrant, forcing a reevaluation of Mavuno's engagement strategy with them. This would also be a good time to evaluate the deployed engagement strategies for each quadrant.

Conclusion

While SE is beginning to reach a broad scholarly audience and warrants for cross-disciplinary research (Short et al., 2009), there is still no study on SE that consider how to communicate with various actors in the field. We hope that our article and accompanying exercise will stimulate work in this area and provide a helpful guide for SE who are launching their ventures.

References and Additional Resources

Alvord, S.H., L.D. Brown, and C.W. Letts. 2004. "Social Entrepreneurship and Societal Transformation an Exploratory Study." *Journal of Applied Behavioral Science* 40, no. 3, pp. 260–82.

Bacq, S., and F. Janssen. 2011. "The Multiple Faces of Social Entrepreneurship: A Review of Definitional Issues Based on Geographical and Thematic Criteria." *Entrepreneurship & Regional Development* 23, nos. 5–6, pp. 373–403.

Bain & Company, Inc. 2014. "Growing Prosperity: Developing Repeatable Models to Scale the Adoption of Agricultural Innovations." Bain report with the collaboration of Acumen Fund available at www.bain.com/publications/business-insights/growing-prosperity.aspx retrieved March 2014.

Borzaga, C., and S. Sacchetti. 2015. "Why Social Enterprises Are Asking to Be Multi-stakeholder and Deliberative: An Explanation Around the Costs of Exclusion." Euricse Working Papers 75, no. 15.

Carroll, A.B. 1989. *Business and Society: Ethics and Stakeholder Management.* Cincinnati, OH: South-Western Publishing.

Cornelissen, J. 2011. *Corporate Communication: A Guide to Theory and Practice,* 3rd ed. Thousand Oaks, CA: Sage.

Cornelissen, J. 2011. "Stakeholder Management and Communication." In *Corporate Communication: A Guide to Theory and Practice,* ed. J. Cornelissen, 39–58. 3rd ed. Thousand Oaks, CA: Sage.

Dacin, P.A., M.T. Dacin, and M. Matear. 2010. "Social Entrepreneurship: Why we Don't Need a New Theory and How We Move Forward from Here." *Academy of Management Perspectives* 24, no. 3, pp. 37–57.

Defourny, J., and M. Nyssens. 2006. "Defining Social Enterprise." In *Social Enterprise,* ed. M. Nyssens, 3–26. Oxon: Routledge Publishing.

Di Domenico, M.L., H. Haugh, and P. Tracey. 2010. "Social Bricolage: Theorizing Social Value Creation in Social Enterprise." *Entrepreneurship, Theory and Practice* 34, no. 4, pp. 681–703.

Dorado, S. 2006. "Social Entrepreneurial Ventures: Different Values So Different Processes of Creation, No?" *Journal of Developmental Entrepreneurship* 11, no. 4, pp. 319–43.

Dorigo, L., and G. Marcon. 2014. "A Caring Interpretation of Stakeholder Management for the Social Enterprise. Evidence from a Regional Survey of Micro Social Co-Operatives in the Italian Welfare Mix." WP 1/2014, Working Paper series, Universita Ca' Foscari Venezia, ISSN: 2239-2734.

Elmes, B., S. Juisto, G. Whiteman, R. Hersh, and G. Gunthey. 2012. "Teaching Social Entrepreneurship and Innovation from the Perspective of Place and Place Making." *Academy of Management Learning & Education* 11, no. 4, pp. 533–54.

Freeman, R.E. 1984. *Strategic Management: A stakeholder Approach.* Boston: Pitman.

Fritz, V., B. Levy, and R. Ort, eds. 2014. *Problem-Driven Political Economy Analysis: The World Bank's Experience.* World Bank Publications.

Haugh, H. 2007. "Community-Led Social Venture Creation." *Entrepreneurship Theory and Practice* 31, no. 2, pp. 161–82.

Howorth, C., S.M. Smith, and C. Parkinson. 2012. "Social Learning and Social Entrepreneurship Education." *Academy of Management Learning & Education* 11, no. 3, pp. 371–89.

Ilies, R., T. Judge, and D. Wagner. 2006. "Making Sense of Motivational Leadership: The Trail from Transformational Leaders to Motivated Followers." *Journal of Leadership and Organizational Studies* 13, no. 1, pp. 1–22.

Kanter, R., and D. Summers. 1987. "Doing Well While Doing Good: Dilemmas of Performance Measurement in Nonprofit Organizations and the Need for a Multiple-Constituency Approach." In *The Nonprofit Sector: A Research Handbook,* ed. W.W. Powell, 154–66. New Haven: Yale University Press.

Litzky, B.E., V. Godshalk, and C. Walton-Bongers. 2009. "Social Entrepreneurship and Community Leadership: A Service-Learning Model for Management Education." *Journal of Management Education* 34, no. 1 pp. 142–62.

Lovejoy, K., and G. Saxton. 2012. "Information, Community, and Action: How Nonprofit Organizations Use Social Media." *Journal of Computer-Mediated Communication* 17, no. 3, pp. 337–53.

Lovejoy, K., R. Waters, and G. Saxton. 2012. "Engaging Stakeholders through Twitter: How Nonprofit Organizations are Getting More out of 140 Characters or Less." *Public Relations Review* 38, no. 2, pp. 313–18.

Marcon, G., and L. Dorigo. 2012. "Stakeholder Theory and Care Management: An Inquiry into Social Enterprises." WP 21/2012, Working Paper series, Universita Ca' Foscari Venezia, ISSN: 2239-2734.

Miller, T.L., C.L. Wesley, and D. Williams. 2012. "Educating the Minds of Caring Hearts: Comparing the Views of Practitioners and Educators on the Importance of Social Entrepreneurship Competencies." *Academy of Management Learning & Education* 11, no. 3, pp. 349–70.

Preston, L.E., and H.T. Sapienza. 1990. "Stakeholder Management and Corporate Performance." *Journal of Behavioral Economics* 19, pp. 361–75.

Russel, R. 2004. "What Works. Pumping Prosperity." *Sanford Social Innovation Review* (Winter), pp. 51–52.

Wei-Skillern, J., J. Austin, H. Leonard, and H. Stevenson. 2007. *Entrepreneurship in the Social Sector.* Thousand Oaks: Sage Publications.

Zahra, S.A., E. Gedajlovic, D.O. Neubaum, and J.M. Shulman. 2009. "A Typology of Social Entrepreneurs: Motives, Search Processes and Ethical Challenges." *Journal of Business Venturing* 24, no. 5, pp. 519–32.

CHAPTER 14

Marketing a Social Enterprise: Generating Questions to Construct Observation Experiences

Mary Conway Dato-on

Crummer Graduate School of Business, Rollins College

Introduction

In designing marketing or communication strategies, students often rush in to offer suggestions to social entrepreneurs prior to fully appreciating the breadth and depth of the organization's challenges and context. Rushing to solve social-related problems often demonstrates a lack of empathy for social entrepreneurs' and their clients' struggles. When this occurs, resulting suggestions and marketing plans are often unrealistic or mismatched with organizational needs—resulting in frustration and ultimately failure to improve outcomes. At the same time, social entrepreneurs often do not fully understand the need for marketing plans or strategies with social goals since their focus is on creating (not communicating) social goals. This exercise develops steps students can use to analyze the situation through the use of human-centered design thinking approaches to environmental analysis—internal and external to the organization. The activity also provides a platform for the instructor to connect the importance of focusing on marketing an organization's social mission, process, outcomes, and impact to various stakeholders.

Purpose

This exercise is designed to teach the first stages of human-centered design thinking: HEAR. While this initial phase is one of observation and usually based in the field, instructors are often limited in the capacity to take students into the field. As such, this exercise is designed to connect students to social entrepreneurs who visit their classroom (physically or virtually) and generate interface questioning in a way that enables students to hear the voice of the social entrepreneur working in the field.

Learning Objectives

- Practice first stage of human-centered design thinking—HEAR
- Engage with active social entrepreneurs to improve primary research gathering techniques while learning about focal organizations marketing
- Compare theoretical readings on social enterprise and nonprofit marketing to actual practice
- Develop reporting and summarizing skills (oral and written) based on exercise findings

Exercise

The exercise is broken into four parts: introductions, interactions, reporting, and debriefing. The class format is small group discussions with students reporting findings to the entire class. Instructor-led debriefing enables learning across the different marketing topics with social focus, thus facilitating depth and breadth of learning.

Schedule: Based on a 1.5-hour class session

- 10 to 15 min introductions
- 30 to 40 min small group Q and A with assigned social enterprise members
- 20 to 25 min debrief from each group to the entire class
- 10 to 20 min wrap-up and connection back to human-centered design thinking principles and social entrepreneurial practices (e.g., why marketing, communication, and branding activities matter to a social entrepreneur and a social enterprise)

Set-up: The instructor will need to arrange with one of more social entrepreneurs who are actively involved in running a social enterprise to attend class (physically or virtually).

- *Preparing the entrepreneurs:* Give specific instructors to visitors regarding the time they will have to introduce the organization and themselves (recommend 5 minutes maximum since students have already conducted secondary research). Ensure visitors understand the purpose of the exercise (e.g., learning objectives) and what, if anything, they can expect to receive from the experience (e.g., organizational exposure, feedback on the organization's marketing, a formal report). Emphasize the need for frankness in responses to student inquiries and safeguard any confidentiality needed to make the visitors feel comfortable in disclosing information (e.g., are nondisclosure agreements necessary?). The instructor should also decide (and prearrange with visiting entrepreneurs) whether they will be present for the debrief or receive a more formal feedback at a later date.
- *Preparing questions:* Depending on course level (i.e., graduate, undergraduate) and focus (i.e., introductory, upper-level), instructors may have student teams generate the questions based on assigned readings and research. Alternatively, the instructor may provide guiding questions that will help the students begin the interview and cover required topics (see teaching notes for example).
- *Preparing the students:* Prereading should be given (see teaching notes) on the concepts of human-centered design thinking and marketing in nonprofit and social enterprises. It is also helpful if students conduct preliminary research on the visiting entrepreneurs' organization and the people themselves. View organizations' websites, social media, videos, and annual reports to assess what the organization says about itself and investigate what others say about it (e.g., nonprofit rating agencies, news coverage). Ensure the students know they will be required to debrief the interview to the entire class and explain any requirements for the debrief (e.g., timing, key points to cover).

- *Options:* The instructor may choose to focus on one organization and invite several key players and clients (if possible/appropriate) to share various viewpoints on the questions students ask. Alternatively, the same questions can be asked across organizations and student teams and comparisons made.

1. *Introductions:* The focal social enterprise(s) present the vision, mission, and current operations. This should supplement any pre-reading the instructor has assigned student research on the organization(s).
2. *Interactions:* Student teams of three to four meet with assigned social enterprise members. To enhance focus, separate rooms or large physical distance between teams should be maintained. Students should quickly introduce themselves and begin the interview based on pre-reading, prior research, and assigned or developed questions.
3. *Reporting:* After interview with visiting entrepreneurs, students return to the larger class. Each team is given 5 to 8 minutes (depending on number of teams and allotted time) to explain the learning from the interview based on questions asked and in comparison to pre-reading and their own research. The instructor may give specific debrief points to cover or allow for free-flow presentations.
4. *Debriefing:* Instructors use this time to connect the experiences across the different organizations or enterprise players and probe the relationship between pre-reading and research/interview findings. Key to learning in this process is that students focus on **hearing** the entrepreneurs rather than jumping to conclusions and offering suggestions. This hearing requires empathy and patience and is essential to the difference between failure and success in client interaction and consulting.

CHAPTER 15

Soup-On-The-Go: Joni's Soup Fellowship

Jennifer S.A. Leigh

Nazareth College

Summary

This mini-case introduces a grassroots soup kitchen in rural Maine with the potential to become a small-scale social enterprise. The narrative describes the founder's efforts to build community by addressing food insecurity issues. Topics covered in the case include brief background information on the founder, the economic context, key stakeholders, challenges, and opportunities.

Learning Objectives

- To diagnose a grassroots entity using the social lean or business model canvas.
- Apply findings from the social lean/business model canvas to brainstorm and then evaluate potential social enterprise business models.

Assignment

- Prework: There is no prework for this assignment given that the case is short enough to read in class.
- Postwork: Legal Structure Assignment—Select a social enterprise legal structure available in your country that best matches the business model for a small-scale "soup kitchen"

organization with a similar mission to the one in this case. Prepare a one page (or less) paper discussing why you selected this legal structure and the pros and cons of the model.

Case

1. Introduction: Joni's Soup

"Should I cook cream of corn or chicken noodle soup this time?" Joni asked me as we spoke on the phone during our weekly conversation. Joni, a 72-year-old "new" retiree, had recently started her "second act"—a monthly soup for patrons of a local food pantry in rural Maine named Soup-On-The-Go. "They liked the chicken soup last time, but I want to try something different and one of my volunteers is a vegetarian, so I don't want to offend her."

2. The vision

Joni had a strong commitment to serve those in her community— through her paid and unpaid work. Her vision upon retirement was to build upon the services at the local food pantry at her former church where she volunteered regularly. She noticed three patterns. First, many of the older patrons who used the services came early and often socialized before the food pantry formally opened. Second, she had seen that working families often rushed after work and often in between jobs to get to the pantry with cranky and hungry children with them. Third, after the pantry started receiving fresh produce from a state grant, many patrons couldn't even identify vegetables in their natural forms. "How can we expect people to use these vegetables if they don't know how to cook them?" It is from these observations that her initiative sprung forth: "I will use the same whole food ingredients to make the soups and this will demonstrate to people how they might use the veggies!"

Initially Joni had planned to develop the project with her best friend; however, health issues soon limited her ability to participate regularly. Joni began by sharing the idea with the Episcopalian priest at her former church, which housed a local food pantry open to the entire community. Joni's local food pantry reflected the typical U.S. trend—faith-based organizations sponsor of 62 percent of food pantries as part of their community outreach (Weinfield 2014). The priest loved the idea, but she needed vestry (church governance) approval since the facility was already being used for the church's fish chowder fundraisers during other parts of the year.

Financing the soup components was another concern. The fresh produce grant from the state wanted her to charge a nominal amount for the soup. This bothered Joni, who wanted to provide a free service and felt that charging would interfere with the welcoming environment she hoped to create. Likewise, the priest disliked charging a fee on religious grounds since she viewed hosting the soup kitchen as part of their outreach ministry and the Christian mandate to serve the poor.

3. Economic context: The state and the community

Maine, located in the uppermost east coast of the United States, is a small, rural state with a declining and aging population of approximately 1.3 million people and a 5 percent unemployment rate as of February 2015. This unemployment figure tracks close to the national average of 5.5 percent. U.S. Census data reported that the percentage of people in Maine living in poverty at 13.6 percent, which is slightly below the national average of 15.4 percent (U.S. Census Bureau 2015). More detailed regional analysis for this region of the state reveals a steady increase in the number of families participating in national food-related welfare programs. This is reflected in the rising number of households in the SNAP program (government-subsidized food assistance) from 1,319 in 2002 to 2,957 households in 2010, as well as a growing percentage of students eligible for free and reduced lunch in public schools: 32 percent in 2002 up to 41.7 percent in 2010 (Acheson 2010). These national programs are designed to address food insecurity and the families who enjoy Joni's soup are representative of these statistics.

4. Start up

"I don't know how I had time for work before retirement," Joni quipped during a phone interview. "Between the soup project, bringing people to the doctors, having my former colleague's girls, and visiting people I don't know where the days go." In addition to the half-year once-a-month soup project, Joni worked two days a week doing elder care, supported her long-time best friend with a number of medical issues, and acted as an informal great-aunt role for one of her former colleagues' children. Fortunately, when she was out and about in the community for these other activities, she could pick up additional veggies or other resources donated by friends or contacts at local shops.

5. Everybody knows Joni

Joni had worked for over 25 years in the local school system as an Educational Tech II, otherwise known as a teacher's aide. In this capacity, she got to know generations of teachers, students, and their families. In addition, working with high-needs students with challenging intellectual disabilities, she sought to identify opportunities for her students to gain practical knowledge in local organizations and life skills to ensure their dignity as adults. To create these connections, she often interacted with numerous small businesses, nonprofits, and community-based organizations.

At home, her jobs, and her community organizations, Joni was always in charge of food. Joni and her husband bought a 200-year-old farmhouse as part of the back to the land movement in the 1970s. There they raised two children and two massive vegetable gardens, as well as a rotation of various poultry—most famously turkeys. Like generations of thrifty and frugal New Englanders before her, every summer she harvested, canned, and composted the very few vegetable scraps. "I had 6 brothers and sisters so I knew how to make food stretch." At work Joni organized most of the community celebrations for life cycle events—weddings, retirements, and new babies. She had earned the reputation of the frugal Martha Stewart and her colleagues looked forward to her economical and creative food.

Before her employment with the school system, she had a kaleidoscope career working as an administrative assistant in a doctor's office, in a seasonal fast food restaurant, at a local corner store, and as full-time homemaker. In all of these roles, she established a web of connections within her community and her natural extroversion certainly helped her networking abilities. Her children had joked that she could take an airplane ride and arrive in a new city with three new best friends.

6. Serving soup and fellowship

For the first 2 years, Joni adopted a "small is beautiful" philosophy and committed to serving a very streamlined menu, like most soup kitchens, but only 6 months of the year from September to March once a month on Thursdays during the food pantry evening. "In Maine in the winter you have to be efficient," Joni reminded me, "you have to get the food, so you might as well have a soup option. Soup and bread—that's it."

On an average soup fellowship night at Soup-On-The-Go, Joni and her volunteers make two big 20 quart pots and serve approximately 30 bowls. "It's hard to give an exact number," remarked Joni, "because sometimes there are seconds and sometimes the church choir who sing show tunes during the event gets some soup, too." Typically, she and her volunteers prepare about 10 to 15 quarts in mason jars or other recycled glass jars for "take-out." There's lots of variation based on the soup and the weather as winters bring cold temperatures and frequent snow storms in that region. Overall about ½ to ⅓ of those attending the food pantry participate in the soup fellowship, again depending on the menu and weather.

Occasionally someone from the community would come because they've read about it from one of the flyers Joni posted in the community. She advertised the event with modest posters on bulletin boards at grocery stores, laundromats, government offices where people apply for public assistance, thrift store and churches. "I'm happy when someone came from the notices because the idea is for it to be something for more people—for community building, networking, and building connections."

For the first 2 years, Joni relied on donations from a small group of family and friends who functioned as patrons and bought the ingredients based upon a pre-agreed upon list that she provided. Recently, this agreement has ended amicably because one of the donors was taking a new job that limited her contribution ability.

Until this change Joni shared she didn't really know the cost because that was handled by the group. Based on discussions with the donors, she learned that the average costs ran between $75 and $100 for each soup night depending on the ingredients and what she could, in her words, glean from her friend's gardens. Occasionally people who know about the soup call me up and say, "Joni—Do you want some potatoes? I have a lot right now. So I try to incorporate those into the meal." These included former colleagues, friends, church members, neighbors, and local farmers.

Recently, Mandy, a long-time volunteer with the food pantry in her mid-thirties, approached Joni about getting more involved in the Soup-On-The-Go. Mandy saw potential to connect the soup night with a local version of soup projects like The Women's Bean Project. Joni recalled a similar product produced in Rochester, NY, and reflected on this possibility and Mandy's other strengths: She could bring new skills and connections to the project from her experiences as a small business owner selling produce and products from her local organic farm, in addition to understanding the food pantry clients.

7. What's on your plate?

With the loss of her patrons, Joni created her first e-mail soliciting financial support (see following box) with the idea of approaching people in her networks—her book club, the church where the program is located, and other civic and community groups (i.e., scouting troops, sorority organizations, business groups). While the funding situation remained unclear, Joni also had to consider opportunities for growth. Besides Mandy's interest in joining the organizing team, a town official had approached her about expanding the program at the municipal building as part of their initiative to support sharing economy initiatives. Gretchen, the manager of the food pantry, had encouraged Joni to come with her to more food pantry network meetings and trainings to learn more about the issues and organizations involved in food programs at the state level. In attending previous meetings with Gretchen, Joni realized that she would shortly need to address the issue of legal status to manage finances since she did not want to rely on funds going through the church.

With fall fast approaching, Joni reflected about the next steps for the Soup-On-The-Go initiative:

I've learned so much organizing soup nights and at the same time I feel I need more help organizing and I wish I had more flexibility to see my grandchildren out of state during the school year. I'll just have to see what the universe has planned for soup night and me!

Discussion Questions

Diagnose Soup-On-The-Go with the social lean canvas (http://sociallean-canvas.com/) or the business model canvas. (www.businessmodelgenera-tion.com/downloads/business_model_canvas_poster.pdf)

Based on the canvas diagnosis, answer the following questions:

- What do you see as *the* main challenge facing Help-Yourself Soup-On-The-Go? Why?
- What are the causes? What are some solutions?

How could Soup-On-The-Go convert from a grassroots effort to a self-financing social enterprise? What products and services align with the resources and relationship identified in the case?

What concerns might the different stakeholders in Soup-On-The-Go have about becoming a social enterprise and how might you address those?

CHAPTER 16

Worksheet for "Recognizing, Pitching, and Communicating Social Opportunities"

Paul Miesing

University at Albany, State University of New York

Beneficiaries

Know Thy Market: For whom are you creating value? How will you increase the beneficiaries served or the amount they purchase?

Target Market = _____

Client Profile = _____

Relationships = _____

Current Offerings = _____

Value Proposition

What will distinguish yours from competing offerings? For instance, will you offer specialized or niche products and services, or locate where competitors ignore?

Unique Product/Service Features = _____

Sustainable Competitive Advantage = _____

Pricing Strategy = _____

Competition

Who else is providing the types of products/services you are proposing?

Competitive Intensity (number of rivals, average profitability, barriers, etc.) = _____

Typical Core Competencies = _____

Assessment of Offerings = _____

Uniqueness = Promotion & Distribution

_____

How will you communicate your product/service offerings?

Marketing & Advertising = _____

Public Relations = _____

Networking = _____

Social Media = _____

Resources

"Writing A (Social) Business Plan"

Woody Allen once quipped that "If show business wasn't a business, it would be called show show." The same can be said of social enterprises: If there was no business component, it would be called "social social." Review the various worksheets you completed for the different topics—these can comprise

the basis of your social business plan. Consider the following outline for presenting and writing it; these merely suggest topics—use discretion in applying them to your specific analysis.

Preliminary Sections
- Cover page
- Table of contents
- Executive summary:
    - ✓ Who is the social entrepreneur and what unique skill, service, or background does he/she/they bring to the venture?
    - ✓ What is the venture and where is it now? Is it truly new and important? Who will benefit from it? How?
    - ✓ Where do you want to go—What will constitute success?
    - ✓ How you will get there—How (in general terms) will the idea be executed?
    - ✓ What kind of support for the enterprise do you need? What resources are required?

The Business Model
- Social purpose/mission statement/aims:
  - ✓ Why is there a need for this social enterprise? Who will benefit? How will you meet the need?
- Products, services, activities, and so on.
- Key innovations or adaptations
- Financial and social goals and objectives:
  - ✓ Definition of success and "value"
  - ✓ How you will measure progress toward "social impact"?
- Ownership/organization:
  - ✓ Legal structure, equity positions, financial deal
- Potential partners and stakeholders
- Starting the enterprise:
  - ✓ Acquiring staff, space, and equipment
  - ✓ When will you deliver services?
- Achieving financial sustainability:
  - ✓ Key milestones/timelines and associated activities
  - ✓ Short-term (can be achieved in less than a year), intermediate (1–3 years), long-term (often require 3–5 years to achieve)
  - ✓ Realistic assessment of chances for success
- Exit strategy (how and when investors will recoup their money):
  - ✓ Sell? Merge with another social venture? Dissolution— mission accomplished?

The Market
- Industry description ("five forces"?)
- The competition (e.g., similar social enterprises) and competitive advantage
- Target segment:
  - ✓ Who will buy your goods/services? Why from you?
  - ✓ Market research (including trends)
  - ✓ Expected position and share

The People
- Key figures:
  - ✓ Leader(s)/founder(s)—Background, education, experience, accomplishments, reputation, skills, character/integrity, motivations/personal drive
  - ✓ Others—Board of Directors, Advisors/Counselors, Consultants
- Human resource management strategy:
  - ✓ The team—from top management to first-line
  - ✓ Key staff (skills, experience, knowledge)

The Marketing Plan
- Revenue model:
  - ✓ Demand management (e.g., pricing and expected surplus)
- Income from for-profit activities versus noncommercial
  - ✓ Communications (e.g., direct mail, media, social networking)
  - ✓ Publicity and showcases
  - ✓ Marketing "the brand"
- E-commerce strategy

The Finance Plan
- Financial needs for 3 to 5 years
- Source(s) for resources
- Methods of fundraising (investment capital, donors, philanthropist/angel, grants, IPO)
- Returns:
  - ✓ Projected income, expenditure, cash flow
  - ✓ Balance sheet; profit and loss
- Financial management systems
- When venture will become financially self-supporting

Risk/Reward Assessment
- Critical risks and contingencies (potential impact of failures, problems, unforeseen events and trends):

✓ Financial, Legal, Talent, Technological, Environmental, Other
- Scenario planning—Best case to worst case

Concluding Sections
- Summary
- Scheduling and milestones (calendar of expected dates and events)

Appendixes
- Supporting documents:
  ✓ Résumés for founders and key enterprise participants
  ✓ References/letters of recommendation (e.g., banker, lawyer, accountant)
  ✓ Sources of data used in the plan, including professional advisers' reports if used
  ✓ References for literature cited in the plan, if any
  ✓ Other (e.g., photographs/drawings, market surveys, web page mock-up, product prototype(s), video, sample press release, etc.)

Overall Appeal
- Feasibility of the plan (e.g., attractiveness of the market opportunity; realistic)
- Alignment of social and financial returns on investment
- Market, operational, and technological viability (e.g., value created by the new product or service; competitive advantage of the proposed venture)
- Keep it simple but clarify, clarify, clarify
  ✓ Is the plan ... comprehensive? Sufficiently analytical? Reasonable?
- Physical appearance (well-written and presented, easy to read, crisp, clean):
  ✓ Check spelling and grammar
  ✓ Have someone else read to check for omissions and weakness

About the Authors

Maria Aggestam's research revolves around such themes as entrepreneurship, social entrepreneurship, environmental jolts, gender, teaching and learning, and include broad spectrum of entrepreneurship related issues. In addition, she is writing about entrepreneuring processes in various industries such as in art-related industries, high-tech industry, biotechnology, social entrepreneurship and recently entrepreneurs within Swedish gastronomy. Her research is cross-disciplinary, combining perspectives from among the social sciences. Her most recent interests include, for example, the relations between language and entrepreneurial achievement within gastronomic domain and also relations between business and society, namely social entrepreneurship. She is research affiliated to Sten K. Johnson Centre for Entrepreneurship at the Department of Business Administration, Lund University but also affiliated to Nelson Mandela African Institution of Science and Technology where she is going to serve on the teaching team on master programme in entrepreneurship and innovation and also as an advisor to start-up enterprises.

Mary Conway Dato-on is a researcher of international business and social entrepreneurship at Rollins College, Crummer Graduate School of Business. She serves as the Change Leader for the Ashoka U Changemaker designation at Rollins. For 2013–2014 she received a Fulbright Garcia-Robles Scholarship to study Social Entrepreneurship in the Mexican Context. She was part of the core team that developed the Global Links Program—a public private partnership with Tupperware Brands and the U.S. Department of State under the Ambassador-at-Large for Global Women's Issues, for which she serves as faculty mentor. She earned her PhD in Marketing from University of Kentucky. Her publishing profile includes a book, numerous journal articles, book chapters, on social entrepreneurship, nonprofit branding, social marketing, cross-cultural consumer behavior, as well as gender and ethics in marketing. Her research has appeared in *The Journal of Business Ethics, Social*

Entrepreneurship Journal, the Journal of Social Enterprise, *The Business Journal of Hispanic Research, Journal of Developmental Entrepreneurship, Journal of Nonprofit and Voluntary Sector Marketing, International Journal of Shopping Center Research, Psychology and Marketing Journal, Journal of Marketing Theory and Practice, Journal of Business-to-Business Marketing,* among others.

Sunny Jeong is a business oriented scholar. she received her PhD at the University of Illinois at Urbana-Champaign. Her teaching area is international business, business in East Asia, and global social entrepreneurship. Her research interests are social and spiritual capital in management and entrepreneurship. She served on the committee of Philanthropic Innovations Forum (Social Entrepreneur Incubator) and was involved in Student Association for Social Entrepreneurship, which host annual social entrepreneurship case competition and workshop since 2012 at the University of Illinois at Urbana-Champaign. She has consulted small- to large-size companies in the USA, Korea, Japan and China. She also advises new social venture development (L3C, 501(C)3 corporation). She led many International Business Plan Competitions concerning sustainability and global social problem. She received an Excellent Volunteer Award and Social Justice Award (at the University of Illinois at Urbana-Champaign), and Excellent Teaching Award (at the Wittenberg University).

Rachida Justo is an entrepreneurship and social entrepreneurship risearcher at IE Business School. Through her professional experience, she has produced state-of-the art academic knowledge and teaching tools that are needed to train social entrepreneurs and help them to create value for their companies. Her research, which focuses on social entrepreneurship and women entrepreneurs has been published in Top-tier international journals such as the *Journal of Business Venturing, Small Business Economics* and *Industrial and Labor Relations Review,* as well as in several books and book chapters. She has also received several awards such as the "Best Women's Entrepreneurship Paper Award" and the "Distinguished Reviewer Award" from the Entrepreneurship division of the Academy of Management, the "Research excellence award" from IE Business School and the "Outstanding Award for Best Doctoral Dissertation" from the

UAM. Her passion for the field of social entrepreneurship has pushed her to engage with different stakeholders that form the social business ecosystem. For example, she collaborates actively with several key players of the Entrepreneurship and social entrepreneurship ecosystem (such as Ashoka Spain, UnLtd and UEIA) in supporting and increasing the visibility of Spanish entrepreneurs and in designing appropriate scaling strategies.

Jerrid P. Kalakay is Co-Founder of LeadUp Innovations, a leadership and organizational development practice based in Orlando, Florida. Currently, he serves as a Leadership and Change Engineer working to improve the processes, systems, and structures within a variety of organizations to maximize their capital wealth and social value creation respectively. He received his doctorate degree in the Leadership and Change from Antioch University; his dissertation research was focused on the incidents that social entrepreneurs identified as critical to leading their enterprises. In service to the community, Jerrid serves on the Board of Directors for the Global Peace Film Festival and as a national trainer for Echoing Green's Work on Purpose Curriculum. He is interested in advancing conversations around the intersections of entrepreneurship, education, and positive social change.

Ashley King-Bischof founded Markit Opportunity, a for-profit social enterprise based in Kenya, in order to improve market access for smallholder farmers across the East African Community. Markit Opportunity was incubated at IE and placed as a finalist in the Impact Weekend and a semifinalist in Venture Day competitions in Spain in 2014. Ashley has worked with various technology startups with a real passion for small businesses and micro-entrepreneurs, including Yelp.com, MyAgro.org and Kiva.org. Additionally, she has consulted various early-stage social enterprises in Latin America, Southeast Asia and Africa. As of October 2015, Markit Opportunity was named the winner of the Barclays Africa Supply Chain Challenge in Cape Town, South Africa, validating its mobile platform.

Jennifer S.A. Leigh is management researcher at Nazareth College of Rochester. She received her PhD in organization studies from the Carroll

School of Management at Boston College. Her scholarship addresses responsible management education, cross-sector social partnerships, and corporate social responsibility. She co-edited the book Educating for Responsible Management: Putting Theory into Practice with Roz Sunley (2016). Jennifer is a Senior Editor for The Annual Review of Social Partnerships (ARSP), an Associate Editor of the Journal of Management Education and Business Ethics: A European Review (BEER), and an editorial board member of the Academy of Management Learning and Education (AMLE).

Rakhi Mehra graduated from Harvard Business School (HBS) in 2009 and previously read Philosophy, Politics & Economics at Oxford University. She co-founded mHS City Labs as an interdisciplinary social enterprise to foster inclusive cities and address low income housing challenges in India. The innovations were recognized by the Clinton Global Initiative with a complementary membership and awarded by the internet.org challenge launched by Facebook. She also received the HBS Social Entrepreneurship Award in 2011. Rakhi has consulted on housing finance with the World Bank and her experience in social innovation, fostering partnership, private sector engagement and policy research spans the nonprofit, for profit and academic sector with University of Bocconi, CARE International, Rabo bank, Grameen Bank and Jeffery Sach's Office at Columbia University.

Paul Miesing is a management and social entrepreneurship scholar. He conducts research and training in various strategic management areas. His current research interests are in social entrepreneurship, environmental sustainability, and corporate governance. He has published dozens of articles and papers in both academic and practitioner journals, including the following Financial Times "top 45" journals: *Academy of Management Journal, California Management Review, Journal of Business Ethics, Journal of Marketing* (among numerous others), and has received a Distinguished Research Award. Prof. Miesing was a Fulbright lecturer at Fudan University in Shanghai and was a Visiting Professor at several other universities around the world. He is in various Who's Who directories and was an Outstanding Young Man of America, past a recipient of American

Assembly of Collegiate Schools of Business (AACSB) Federal Faculty Fellowship. He served on several peer review boards, including the Council for International Exchange of Scholars (CIES) and the National Science Foundation. In 2013, he was the recipient of UAlbany's inaugural Exemplary Community Engagement Awards for both Small Enterprise Economic Development and Going Green Globally programs.

Elizabeth A.M. Searing is a researcher at the Rockefeller School of Public Affairs and Policy at the University of Albany (SUNY). Her primary research focus is in nonprofit and social enterprise ecology, but she also conducts work in financial management, evidence-based policy, the role of social and psychological factors in economic development and policy effectiveness, and applied ethics for the social sciences. She has served as editor on two books, and her articles have been published in peer-reviewed journals such as the *Journal of Economic Behavior and Organization*, *Nonprofit and Voluntary Sector Quarterly*, and *Social Science & Medicine*. Elisabeth is active in professional societies, including as co-founder of the Nonprofit Finance and Financial Management common interest group of the Association for Research on Nonprofit Organizations and Voluntary Action (ARNOVA).

Ushnish Sengupta is currently working on his PhD at the Ontario Institute for Studies in Education (OISE), University of Toronto. He has an Industrial Engineering and MBA education from the University of Toronto, experience in starting up and managing Social Enterprise including Free Geek Toronto, and in delivering entrepreneurship and business courses. His research interests include entrepreneurship, marginalized communities, indigenous communities, and social economy organizations.

Gary Shaheen is working with evidence based employment practices including supported and customized employment, social entrepreneurship in both the public and private sectors that help people with mental illnesses, co-occurring substance abuse disorders and those who are homeless including veterans fully integrate into their communities. Gary is the author of publications such as the Substance Abuse and Mental Health

Administration (SAMHSA)'s "Work as a Priority: A Training Program for Employing People with Psychiatric Disabilities who are Homeless." Gary is a member of the EI Lilly "Community Conversations" national training team, who develops and delivers training on principles, practices and partnerships supporting employment for people with mental illnesses. He also provides training internationally on these topics including projects in Israel, the Netherlands, St. Maarten's, Russia. He is currently working with the Cornell University Program on Employment and Disability.

William Wales is an entrepreneurship scholar at the University at Albany-SUNY. He received his PhD in management from Rensselaer Polytechnic Institute. His research principally explores the concept of firm-level entrepreneurial orientation, strategy-making processes, and behavior. His work has been presented internationally and published within the *Strategic Management Journal, Journal of Management Studies, Entrepreneurship: Theory and Practice, Strategic Entrepreneurship Journal, Journal of Business Research, Journal of Product Innovation Management,* and the *International Small Business Journal* among others.

Alia Weston is a management scholar at OCAD University, Toronto. She has an expertise in the areas of business management and design, and her research is focused on understanding how creativity and business can contribute to positive social change. Key themes in her research include exploring creative resistance within resource constrained environments, and exploring how alternative business practices can contribute to solving key challenges in society. Alia's work has been published in a diverse range of media. This includes scholarly work in *Organization* journal, edited collections on *Critical Perspectives on Entrepreneurship*, and *Precarious Spaces: The Arts, Social & Organizational Change,* as well as the *Globe and Mail* a leading Canadian newspaper. In conjunction with her research she hosts workshops and exhibitions which engage with issues related to creative and sustainable work practices. A notable example is the *(Re)² Reconstructing Resilience,* conference and art exhibition.

Caroline Wigren-Kristoferson is entrepreneurship researcher at Lund University. She holds a doctoral degree in Business Administration from

Jönköping International Business School, Jönköping University in Sweden. She carries out research on entrepreneurship in different contexts, e.g. the academic setting, the health care industry and rural areas. She has a great interest for social entrepreneurship and innovation, regional development and methodological issues. At time being her research focus is on entrepreneurship and embeddedness. She has published in journals such as Action Research Journal, Science and Public Policy, Journal of Technology Transfer, International Journal of Entrepreneurship and Small Business and Journal of Developmental Entrepreneurship.

Additional Readings

Boluk, K.A., and Z. Mottiar. 2014. "Motivations of Social Entrepreneurs: Blurring the Social Contribution and Profits Dichotomy." *Social Enterprise Journal* 10, no. 1, pp. 53–68.

Cornforth, C. 2014. "Understanding and Combating Mission Drift in Social Enterprises." *Social Enterprise Journal* 10, no. 1, pp. 3–20.

Dees, J. 1996. *Social Enterprise Spectrum: Philanthropy to Commerce.* Cambridge, MA: Harvard Business School Press.

Dees, J. 1998. "Enterprising Nonprofits." *Harvard Business* Review 76, no. 1, pp. 54–66.

Fletcher, D. 2006. "Entrepreneurial Processes and the Social Construction of Opportunity." *Entrepreneurship and Regional Development: An International Journal* 18, no. 5, pp. 421–40.

Harding, R. 2004. "Social Enterprise: The New Economic Engine?" *Business Strategy Review* 15, pp. 39–43.

Hockerts, K. 2015. "The Social Entrepreneurial Antecedents Scale (SEAS): A Validation Study." *Social Enterprise Journal* 11, no. 3, pp. 260–80.

Krippendorff, K. 2012. "Fast Exercises To Find Your Purpose And Passion For Work." *Fast Company* (September 26) available at www.fastcompany.com/3001583/fast-exercises-find-your-purpose-and-passion-work?partner=newsletter

Roberts, D., and C. Woods. 2005. "Changing the World on a Shoestring: The Concept of Social Entrepreneurship." *Business Review* (Autumn) 7, no. 1, pp. 45–51.

Sahlman, W.A. 1997. "How to Write a Great Business Plan." *Harvard Business Review* 75, no. 4, pp. 98–108.

Santos, F., A.C. Pache, and C. Birkholtz. 2015. "Making Hybrids Work: An Analysis of Key Success Factors." *California Management Review* 57, no. 3, pp. 36–58.

Smith, R., R. Bell, and H. Watts. 2014. "Personality Trait Differences Between Traditional and Social Entrepreneurs." *Social Enterprise Journal* 10, no. 3, pp. 200–21.

Young, D.R., and C. Kim. 2015. "Can Social Enterprises Remain Sustainable and Mission-Focused? Applying Resiliency Theory." *Social Enterprise Journal* 11, no. 3, pp. 233–59.

Videos

Introduction to Social Enterprises and Social Entrepreneurs

"Everyone a changemaker: Casablanca La Marseillaise"—see www.youtube.com/watch?v=HM-E2H1ChJM where Victor Laszlo suddenly transforms from this almost wimpy guy (white suit?) into the guy who makes the Perfect Gesture. Questions: Could you be Victor? Why was HE the changemaker? What could keep you from doing that? How can you help others to be changemakers to make a room full of Victor Lazslos?

"The New Heroes" available at www.pbs.org/opb/thenewheroes/ is a four-hour series hosted by Robert Redford which tells the dramatic stories of twelve social entrepreneurs

M.E. Porter, "The case for letting business solve social problems," *TED Talk* http://go.ted.com/pI6oRQ (Jun 2013)

The Skoll Foundation, "Social Entrepreneurs: Pioneering Social Change," *YouTube* www.youtube.com/watch?v=jk5LI_WcosQ (Feb 18, 2009)

Recognizing, Pitching, and Communicating Social Opportunities

"First Follower: Leadership Lessons from Dancing Guy" at www.youtube.com/watch?v=fW8amMCVAJQ also, see D. Sivers: How to start a movement at www.ted.com/talks/derek_sivers_how_to_start_a_movement.html

Brainstorming—see video clip from "Twelve Angry Men" (for instance, www.youtube.com/watch?v=nfAbTyAcgpE) and discuss how solutions differed with increasing participation in the deliberative process

Steven Johnson, "Where Good Ideas Come From," *YouTube* www.youtube.com/watch?v=NugRZGDbPFU&feature=related (Sep 17, 2010)

Business Models and Plans

J. Saul, "Measuring Social Impact: Challenges and Opportunities," *YouTube* www.youtube.com/watch?v=4DZ7D4FsJ4Q (Jun 2012)

Web Pages

"30 under 30: Social Entrepreneurs." Forbes (December 17, 2012) available at www.forbes.com/special-report/2012/30-under-30/30-under-30_social.html

"Entrepreneurship Learning Activities" available at www.curriki.org/xwiki/bin/view/Coll_Entrepreneurship1/EntrepreneurshipLearningActivities

"List of social enterprises," Wikipedia available at https://en.wikipedia.org/wiki/List_of_social_enterprises

MacMillan, I.C. and Thompson, J.D. *Worksheet Companion: The Social Entrepreneur's Playbook* available at http://wdp.wharton.upenn.edu/worksheet-companion-the-social-entrepreneurs-playbook/

Skoll Foundation social enterprise awardees at www.skollfoundation.org/skoll-awardees/

Index

This book is a publication in support of the United Nations Principles for Responsible Management Education (PRME), housed in the UN Global Compact Office. The mission of the PRME initiative is to inspire and champion responsible management education, research and thought leadership globally. Please visit www.unprme.org for more information.

The Principles for Responsible Management Education Book Collection is edited through the Center for Responsible Management Education (CRME), a global facilitator for responsible management education and for the individuals and organizations educating responsible managers. Please visit www.responsiblemanagement.net for more information.

—Oliver Laasch, University of Manchester, Collection Editor

- *Personal and Organizational Transformation Towards Sustainability: Walking a Twin Path* by Dorothea Ernst
- *Stop Teaching: Principles and Practices for Responsible Management Education* by Isabel Rimanoczy
- *Teaching Ethics Across the Management Curriculum: Principles and Applications, Volume II* by Kemi Ogunyemi
- *Dark Sides of Business and Higher Education Management, Volume I* by Agata Stachowicz-Stanusch and Gianluigi Mangia
- *Dark Sides of Business and Higher Education Management, Volume II* by Agata Stachowicz-Stanusch and Gianluigi Mangia
- *Teaching Ethics Across the Management Curriculum: Contributing to a Global Paradigm Shift, Volume III* by Kemi Ogunyemi
- *Managing for Responsibility: A Sourcebook for an Alternative Paradigm* by Radha R. Sharma, Merrill Csuri, and Kemi Ogunyemi

Announcing the Business Expert Press Digital Library

Concise e-books business students need for classroom and research

This book can also be purchased in an e-book collection by your library as

- a one-time purchase,
- that is owned forever,
- allows for simultaneous readers,
- has no restrictions on printing, and
- can be downloaded as PDFs from within the library community.

Our digital library collections are a great solution to beat the rising cost of textbooks. E-books can be loaded into their course management systems or onto students' e-book readers.
The **Business Expert Press** digital libraries are very affordable, with no obligation to buy in future years. For more information, please visit **www.businessexpertpress.com/librarians**. To set up a trial in the United States, please email **sales@businessexpertpress.com**.